Cristine
May we listen?

A collection of autobiographical
notes, songs, and poems
(October 14, 1954—October 31, 1974)

Cristine A. Rehwaldt
Edited by Charles A. Rehwaldt

*There is a struggle in all men
between the outside and the
inside—especially in me.*

Scripture quotations are taken from the King James Version of the Bible.

ISBN 0-9666527-0-3

Cristine, May We Listen?

Printed in the United States of America.

Contents

Preface

In 1974 our daughter, Cristine, died at the age of twenty in a car-truck accident. That great loss will always be with us; however, we are blessed by having her songs, diary, journal, and many letters and notes which expressed her inner thoughts and feelings. These have been a great comfort to us. We hope that her writings will be a source of inspiration and encouragement to many others.

We are confident that Cristine would approve our decision to share her writings. At various times she told us that she intended to write a book and showed us a few of her notes. Of course we do not know which of these materials, if any, she would have included. We admit that we were not aware of the nature and extent of her writings. We, probably as most parents, did not really listen to what Cristine was saying. She seemed to feel that no one listened to her ideas, her feelings, and her problems. These thoughts are expressed a number of times in her writings. *"Will anyone listen to me anyway?"* Further persuasion came when we found her statement, *"I have a wish to write things down so that they may be saved and shared."*

To our best knowledge, Cristine started writing when she was about 15 and continued to write until the time of her death. The earliest passage from her notes which can be dated was written on November 20, 1971. She did not date many of her writings until she started her notebook on December 3, 1972. Her last entry in the notebook was on September 24, 1974. We have arranged the undated passages to approximate the sequence in which we think they were written, and we have retained only the dates of the first and the last entries of her autobiographical notes. Several passages are from letters she wrote to friends and relatives. We have included the lyrics to several of her songs, together with the music to *The Beckoning*.

We placed a few poems and miscellaneous statements at the end of this book; several of these pages include photocopies of Cristine's notes.

Knowing a few things about her life may help in understanding her words. She was shy, sensitive, and above all else, deeply religious. She fought and overcame her shyness. Present, but not prominent in her writings, was her beautiful sense of humor. She believed her talents were gifts from God and that they had to be developed and used. Though music filled her life, she tried not to be a slave to it. She once wrote to a friend, "*Yes, I did think you were seriously worried, or maybe 'concerned' is a better word, about me in music. It is a very real danger for me and I've seen it happen to kids. Becoming so tunneled into music that you do nothing else, happens, and it's scary to me 'cause I've done it before and don't wanna do it again.*"

In addition to her training as a young Lutheran, two other activities should be mentioned because of the effect on her religious life. These activities occurred during her high school years, the late '60s and early '70s, a time in our city, St. Cloud, Minnesota, of social tension marked by anti-war protests. It was also the time of the "Jesus Movement" which became part of

Cristine's experience. She participated in an ecumenical Bible study group which became known as The House of Light and she sang with The Messengers, a group that sang folk-gospel songs. Many of her songs were written during this period.

The loneliness and sorrow sometimes expressed in Cristine's writings, including her song lyrics, suggest a side of Cristine we seldom saw. We remember her as a happy person, interested in everything around her. She was blessed with many friends, male and female, young and old. For our family, she was like a solid rock, always dependable, always confident, always sure to say and do the right thing. Her advice and opinions were highly respected by family members. We believe others, outside the family circle, saw her in a similar light. One friend wrote:

> It was a little like a light being on when she was around. Not that she was different or goody-goody, but she was so happy,…It is a rare gift, and always gave me a lift.

There is little doubt in our minds that, at least for a time, Cristine felt that something serious would happen to her. Not only is this expressed in her writings, but also in some of her actions. We recall one incident. About the time she graduated from high school she said,"*Dad, show me how to use your tape recorder.*" After being shown which buttons to push, she went to the basement of our home. About an hour later she returned with the tape. Upon handing it to us she said,"*Dad, label this and put it in a safe place.*" She didn't tell us what was on the tape and we didn't ask. A few months after her death the tape was found and played. About half of the tape consisted of Cristine singing some of her songs. This tape proved to be an important source of Cristine's music needed for the record album which we produced after her death. Cristine wanted to make a record album of her music, but there always seemed to be more urgent things that took priority. With the end of The Messengers and her entering college, did she see that a new chapter in her life was beginning, one with more formal music, symphonies, choral music and the like; did she want a record of the past for her own use? Or did she want to leave a record of her music in case something should happen to her? We will never know. Whatever her reasons, we know she enjoyed making the recording. She signed off in a style typical of Cris. She ended with a short song that goes:

This is the end of this dumb tape.
This is the end of a big mistake.
This is the end; I'm so glad it's done.
This is the end of my night of fun.

Cristine composed *The Beckoning* for *a capella* choir just before her death. The day of her fatal accident, we recall, seemed to be one of the happiest days of her life. On that afternoon she finished assembling 35 copies of the manuscript of *The Beckoning*. She was filled with excitement because she was to hear the St. Cloud State University Choir begin rehearsal of her song the next day. Cristine did not live to hear this beautiful song. It seems that on that day her work was done and the Lord called her according to His Will.

We thank each and every person who helped us in assembling materials for both the record album and this collection of writings. Some provided tape recordings, some shared their letters, some related their personal experiences with Cristine, some sent us photographs, others reviewed her writings. We especially thank Mary Smith Weeks for reviewing Cristine's notes and Lynn Walz for her help in organizing Cristine's music. We are thankful that our sister, Arlene Prigge, now deceased, gave us permission to include her poem. We thank Ann Chmielewski and Barb Raymond for typing the manuscript. Lastly, we thank Dr. Albert Krueger for writing the introduction. We know that many hours, even days and weeks, were spent in the endeavor.

We are confident that Cristine was the author of all the writings that we have ascribed to her. However, due to her untimely death and because her notes are incomplete in this regard, we cannot be absolutely sure of this. If any passage in this collection was not written by Cristine, the author is unknown to us.

Charles and Gloria Rehwaldt, parents
June 1997

Introduction:

A Portrait of Cris as Revealed Through Her Activities and Writings

by Albert H. Krueger, Ph.D.
Professor Emeritus of Psychology
St. Cloud State University
St. Cloud, Minnesota

A Prayer for Guidance

*L*ord, guide my hand, my heart, my mind. Help me to prove worthy of the task I have been asked to do. I have been given the rare privilege of seeing the soul of a very special person. She has left this earth, but the evidence of love and beauty which flowed from her remains with us:

She left behind her innermost thoughts and feelings in her diary.

She left behind a joyous sense of love which she poured into her musical compositions, recordings, and poems.

These have been shared with me so that I might understand and introduce her to others so that they too might share and enjoy. Cris wanted it this way. She recognized that the love that was bursting within her could best be expressed and shared through her music and her writings. She told us in her diary:

> *Empty pages lie ahead and I want to fill them all*
> *with songs . . . I must sing, write, play.*
> *Can I leave anything of value behind . . . ?*

I have a wish to write things down so that they
may be saved and shared.

Lord, help me to write with the kind of delicate tenderness and love needed to describe the spirit of her being.

Lord, help me to select just the right words—words which will be in perfect harmony with the characteristics of this exceptional individual.

And above all, Lord, stay my hand so that I write nothing that might mislead, detract from, or tarnish the beauty she left behind. Let all my words flow from love for thee and for mankind, as did hers.

I ask this in Jesus' name whom she loved so much....

Amen

This world is not conclusion;
A sequel stands beyond,
Invisible as music
But positive, as sound.

Emily Dickenson

Cris:
An Introduction

$\mathcal{W}$ho was this unusual young woman whose life ended so abruptly, so tragically, and so unexpectedly, early in her twentieth year?

Who was this unusual young woman whose death filled the church with shocked mourners?

Who was this unusual young woman at whose funeral strong men wept openly?

Who was this unusual young woman whose death so moved both a college English professor and a relative that each wrote a poem about her?

Did anyone really know her?

Did anyone really understand why her death had such an explosive impact upon their emotions?

I recall vividly the morning when I first heard the news of her death; tears began to roll down my cheeks. Why did her death have this impact upon me as well as on so many others? I was not that close to her. I really didn't know her that well. I saw her at church and occasionally at family gatherings. I heard her sing solo in the church choir. I saw her several times at the gift shop in which she worked part-time. But I had never really gotten to know her. I had never really talked with her. Then why did her death affect me so strongly?

I've struggled with this question for a long time. I have considered all of the *obvious* possible reasons and have rejected each in turn:

> She was beautiful in face and figure, with a delicate yet full-blown beauty.

> Her wide-set eyes were arresting with a rare softness and soulfulness. There was a sad wistfulness about them even when she smiled.

> She was blessed with a magnificent talent for music and a need to share that talent with others.

> She was bright. Her academic record was outstanding.

> She was thoughtful and considerate. She gave her parents little or no cause for concern. She could be classified as an "ideal" daughter in this respect.

> She attended church regularly, was active in most musical groups, and directed the junior choir.

> She seemed to emanate a sense of inner peace and tranquility. One might even say that an aura of "unearthliness" surrounded her. Her spirituality was more evident than her physical being.

These were the characteristics that were most obvious to me; impressive, but certainly not sufficient to justify the impact her death had on my emotions.

How did others perceive her? Comments made by others after her death, some of whom knew her well, some not so well, added a little to my understanding. These comments contained the following descriptive words: "Strength," "Special child," "Bright," "Lovely," "Talented," "Warm," "Vital," "Delightful," "Happy," "Quiet," "Joy," "Creative," "Modest," "Shy," "Bashful." She was all of these—but there was something more than this, something beyond descriptive complimentary words such as these.

A comment made by her former music teacher struck home because of the use of one word not included in the above:

> So softly did she enter my life that no one could have anticipated the overwhelming impact she would have on my life.
> —She brought joy to my life through the joy with which she lived her life.

The word which drew my attention was the word "softly." This hadn't occurred to me previously, but upon reading the comment I recognized that in trying to understand Cris one must keep this word in mind. It spells out so clearly the essence of her being. It implies kindness, love, thoughtfulness, humility, and consideration for the welfare and happiness of others. I later recalled that her father once used this word in reference to Cris. I asked him, after reading her diary, if she had ever discussed her thoughts with the family. His response was "Yes, at times, but she came on so softly with these ideas that we didn't pay too much attention." This is sad but understandable. How many of us really listen to our children, particularly when they come on "softly"?

On my request, four people who had been privileged to relate closely with Cris brought additional insight. Her parents stated:

She brought much joy, much laughter, much love, and she taught us many things. She based her life on the conviction that talents and life itself are God-given and are to be used to help others. From early in life she knew she had been given unusual talents. She felt she had to develop these talents and use them in the service of God.

Her older brother added the following succinct but keenly insightful comment:

Gifted to feel and express beauty; burdened with our human frailties. Propelled forward by love; held back by fear. Nevertheless, she served and gave of herself, a child of God.

And finally, the following intriguing statement from a young man, a special friend:

You know a child's joy in spring—that's Cris, but not quite. Although she wanted to be. You know the deep coolness of a shaded summer pool— that's her thoughts, but not quite. You see, she was Cris.

Each of the above stresses a facet or facets of her personality as seen by a number of individuals and each could be considered separately. The real significance of these statements lies in their totality, however. And what they stress is the godliness and the uniqueness of this young woman. She was markedly different. Little more need be said.

All of the observations made by those who knew Cris have been helpful, but to understand her fully, if complete understanding is even possible, one must turn to her writings, including the lyrics of her musical compositions. It was in these that she lay bare her soul. Only in her writings was she able to express her innermost thoughts and feelings. It is only in her writings, for example, that we are exposed to the spiritual, mental, and emotional struggle which at times led her to the brink of exhaustion and caused her to contemplate with longing a period of arrested life. In an undated diary entry, she says:

> *To die...to rest...peace. To be as a tree which can rest for a season and then come back to life— this I wish for. But one cannot die and then return; one must continue on.*

From a careful study of her writings emerges the central theme of her life, particularly in her last three years. These years were dedicated to a search for love, for light, for truth, for trust, for peace. A search which led her to the top of the exhilarating peaks of music, down into the disappointing valley of man and the world, and finally into the satisfying and loving arms of God. Thus was completed a circle, for this search which terminated with God had begun with God. She recognized this, for an isolated line found in her writings states:

> *I search for what I have already found.*

Cris—Music—People—God

Cris' exceptional talent in music goes unquestioned. Hers was a multi-faceted talent encompassing the most vital areas of musical artistry and creativity: instrumental, voice, and composition. The instrument she chose was the violin, probably the most difficult instrument of all to master. But master it she did, taking the Concert Mistress position in the junior and senior high school orchestras for five years and in the college-community orchestra for two-and-one-half years. Her violin performances over the last four years of her life totaled over seventy-five. Her group and solo performances as a vocalist totaled well over one hundred. And her musical compositions approximate forty. On the basis of this evidence alone, one might predict with a good deal of confidence that music would become the first priority in her life. And by man's standards, this would have been a wise and justifiable choice. But Cris did not live by man's standards nor did she make decisions thereby. In an undated diary entry she states:

*I can no longer follow the things man chooses for
me to do—I must follow God's rules.*

This does not mean that she neglected music and allowed
her talents to wither. It does mean, however, that she viewed her
talent as a wondrous gift of God which was to be used for His
glorification, not to gratify her human vanity. In a letter to a
young man she had been dating, she wrote just ten months prior
to her death:

*Don't worry about me working too hard on music.
Granted I get pretty sick of rehearsals all the
time, but deep down I love it very much. And I
learned a long time ago that life is more important
than just music—that's when God became the
most important, and He still is!*

And one month later, an entry found in her diary illustrates
strikingly her desire to serve her Lord and God through music.
She was to sing a solo on the following evening, and her prayer
was that God help her to serve through that song. That night
she prayed:

*Tomorrow I sing and God must touch that song.
Lord, let me serve! You, the music, and the people. Let me be a light for one night—a focused,
directed light—beautiful by your grace. Thank
you, Lord.*

To encounter thoughts and feelings such as these today is rare
and generally comes as a surprise; to encounter such thoughts

and feelings in a person who has not yet reached the age of twenty is both inspiring and humbling.

So, for the glory of God and the service of man, she worked diligently at her music, practicing, performing, composing, until her final day on earth, completing a complex choral composition just a few days before her death. She never heard her final composition because she died the day before it was scheduled to be sung by the college concert choir. This circumstance would have gone unnoticed if the composition had been an "ordinary" composition. Because of the unusual title and lyrics at this particular point in time, however, one is tempted to ask the obvious question: Were her death and the completion of this composition just a coincidence or had God planned it that way? We don't know; we know only that she was happy and at peace with herself, with God, and with the world on those last days. We know that on the day of her death she told her mother that her faith in God had fully matured. We know that, if called, she was prepared to meet her Maker. Ponder carefully the title and words of her final composition, and decide for yourself whether or not you can accept this strange circumstance as mere coincidence:

The Beckoning

Listen to the call of the Lord
    and He shall fill thy heart with many things.
Listen to the call of the Lord
    and He shall fill thy heart with many glorious
    things.
Then shall all treasures overflow
    and shall all emptiness fade away.
And He shall fill thy heart with light
    and joy shall reign.
There shall be light and joy shall reign.
    Hear the call of the Lord.
        Hear the call of the Lord.

Had she seen the Lord beckoning to her? Had she heard Him call? We will never know the answers to these questions but we have sufficient cause to wonder.

Cris—People—God

*P*artially due to her innate temperament, partially due to her sensitive and rather shy nature, partially due to her keen intellectual perception, Cris was unable to find the kind of satisfaction her heart longed for in her relationships with people. Although she enjoyed a close, warm, secure relationship with those within the immediate family circle, her relationship with most others was rather guarded, surface, and emotionally ungratifying. Nevertheless, people did play a vital role in her life—but in a most unusual way. She wanted desperately to love people, to give of herself to them, to develop close, warm, lasting relationships with them, but this she found difficult to achieve. Not that she didn't make friends among her peers; she did—many of them. Not that she didn't develop a close working relationship with teachers and other significant adults; she did—and they thought highly of her. But she seemed unable to give of her intimate self to others. As indicated previously, perhaps this inability was due somewhat to her highly sensitive nature. Her parents relate that when she was in her early teens and shopping with her mother, she had to be "forced" to face the store clerk in order to complete a purchase on her own. Or perhaps it was partially due to her basically shy nature. Her first violin teacher and sixth grade orchestra director stated: "She uttered very few words to me that entire year—five of them were, 'You've spelled my name wrong'." And perhaps it was due to her sharp intellectual perception and her ability to spot shallowness and phoniness, qualities in others she was unable to accept. Whatever the reason, although she longed for a close, lasting emotional relationship with others, she found that this was beyond her grasp.

It wasn't until the last five years that she became actively involved with people, her previous years having been devoted primarily to study, to work, to play, and to quiet introspection. It was her last five years that were amazingly productive and for which a rather definitive record of her thoughts, her fears, her joys, and her sorrows exists. There was approximately a three year period of "public ministry" during this five year span, a period of disappointment, a point of rejection of artificiality in institutionalized worship, and a final period of peace and waiting. And, like Christ, although she walked among them, she was never really one of them; in spirit she was apart—with God. Her diary entry at age eighteen on 12/4/72 states:

There are many around me but my spirit is alone.

The event which drew Cris out of her world of solitude and into the life of others occurred when she was fifteen; she was asked to join a Gospel singing group of young women and men who called themselves The Messengers. The mission of The Messengers was to share Christ's word through song, testimony and discussion. Cris spent nearly three years with this small group. It is this period of her life which I referred to as her "public ministry" because during these years the group sang and talked with more than ninety youth groups. In addition to singing and playing the guitar, Cris composed songs for the group—lovely songs like *Life On A Swing*. The impact made upon young people by this group must have been tremendous because, like Cris, the other members of the group were physically attractive, well groomed, and sincerely religious.

Cris gave fully of herself to this "ministry" for nearly three years, happy that she was bringing the love of God to troubled youth. In a letter to her Grandmother, with whom she corresponded regularly, she wrote on 3/21/72:

> *The Messengers have been really busy lately. We have two or three dates a week now. We're learning about how important it is to sit down and talk with kids and share Scriptures with them after we sing. Kids turn to drugs and sex because they're lonely for love. Only God can fill that loneliness.*

Working with The Messengers, bringing the love of Jesus to many through song and discussion, was a vital experience for Cris. It was during this period in her life that she was able to get relatively close to people and to reveal to them the love that was bursting within her. Although written a few months following the disbandment of The Messengers, she gave recognition to this in a diary entry dated 12/4/72:

> *Yes, we the chosen must pour in our love. I want to pour in my love, so that they may know what I cannot tell them any other way.*

And in an entry made a month prior to this she expressed the fundamental belief on which her witnessing was based:

I'm not a hard core witnesser. Letting Him shine is a lot more important than a lot of words. I hope He does shine. I want Him to. Above all else I want to be His.

The breakup of The Messengers as a witnessing group was inevitable. Unfortunately, other interests began to compete for the time of some of the members. This came as a disappointment to Cris and it may have helped convince her for all time that she could not place her trust in man, only in God. A number of diary entries made shortly after the breakup testify to this attitude toward people. On 11/3/72 she stated:

I don't understand people or friendship. Friends when they need me, gone when they don't.

And on 11/21/72 she observed:

I make friends easily—laugh—gossip. Yet they don't matter. I cannot trust them in the end. They fall away. They don't understand. Only God remains.
A bridge—there is none—I am alone.

Finally, on 12/8/72, she remarked:

People mean little to me anymore. People don't seem real—they are so far away, and I can never trust them. No—they are distant from me—even the closest ones. Surface—everything is surface and cold and artificial.

Spanning approximately the same period of her life as her years with The Messengers was her involvement with a non-denominational youth group known as The Lighthouse, later as The House of Light. This group was devoted primarily to Bible study and discussion and eventually to the more esoteric Biblical events such as healing and prophesy. This filled a need in her life at the time since she was searching for meaning, and the warmth and discussion in such a group may have helped to facilitate her search. She also developed a close relationship with a young man in this group which could well be classified as her first "romantic love." Her involvement with the group eventually terminated, however, and like her experience with The Messengers proved in the end to be a disappointment. It was at this point in her life that she began to differentiate sharply between "man-made" things in Christianity as opposed to the fundamental truths for which Christ lived and died. Unfortunately, The House of Light, which had good intentions, became mired in the relatively unimportant matters of the Biblical story. Cris points this out in a letter to a friend dated 7/8/72:

> *Pray for The House of Light, _____. There are many difficulties and divisions. God forgive me for scorning them. There are people there and I must love them not scorn them or turn them away. I think the problems are very big. They've lost the simplicity of Christ.*

Disappointed and disillusioned for a time she nevertheless continued to love her fellow man. The priorities, however, were never forgotten: "Thou shalt love the Lord thy God with all thy heart, with all thy soul, and with all thy mind…." This became basic with Cris, chiseled deeply into the structure of her being.

In the years following her involvement with The Messengers and The House of Light, Cris immersed herself in college academic work, particularly music in which she was majoring, church activities, and giving of her precious time to troubled peers, individually. As usual, she cast herself fully into these activities, pushing herself to the point of exhaustion. On 4/10/74, just six months before her death, she said in her diary:

> *I worry all the time now. There is a constant tension in everything. I'm so tired and my head aches so often. So tired of "taking time" which everyone advises me—there's never any rest. An hour of nothing is filled with guilt—so I delve into something else. There's no time for fun or just for laughs. I fall into bed at night, exhausted, and can't sleep for the things in my mind; often shed tears.*

No one, including her parents, was aware of the strain under which she was laboring at this time. The soft smile was still on her face and the willingness to help others was undiminished.

Her "public ministry" ended with the breakup of The Messengers; then, it seems that, like the pattern set by Christ, her "private ministry" continued. Her parents reveal that young friends came to see her at the house at any time of the day or night. They came to talk about their problems, but mostly they came to discuss the role of Jesus in their lives and to pray together for guidance. Cris continued this "private ministry" until the day of her death.

Although people often were a disappointment to her, she indicates in her diary on 12/5/72,

> *Human words are sometimes full, but more often*
> *empty, full only of the trivial—they leave me*
> *empty and searching;*

yet, there were some very special people in her life. First and foremost were her parents. Naturally, she was very close to her mother from whom she inherited her physical appearance and her musical talent. Her personality, however, more closely matched that of her father. Like him, she was shy, reserved, methodical, softly but sharply intellectual. From both she inherited, learned, and developed a deep sense of compassion and love for God and man and a willingness to walk the extra mile to help others.

One of the few really "earthy" entries in her diary, spelling out the qualifications she desired in a husband, is a fairly close portrait of her father. Cris paints this picture in an entry made on 1/6/73:

> *And a man whom I can cook for, who likes kids*
> *and good hard work, and who likes to play cards,*
> *drink beer and go fishing. Also, who wears flannel*
> *shirts and blue jeans, likes to go for walks in the*
> *woods and will sit and listen to me sing; and who*
> *will read the Bible for family devotions.*

Similarly, although she seemed quite unaware of it, she had learned from her mother's example, the role of the Christian woman in marriage. In a letter to a friend dated 7/8/72, she says:

> *The Bible is being opened up to me. I've been*
> *learning what it is to be a woman in the kingdom of*

*God. We, being women, have a very special place
in God's kingdom. A man has a natural instinct to
be the head of the house. Women are to be a help-
mate. That doesn't mean that we're his servant or
that we're inferior. It's simply that we're different
and we must fit into God's natural order of things.
If we try to overcome these natural things, we can
totally destroy marriage. If a woman becomes
domineering and independent, it takes away from
the husband and destroys a part of him. Marriage
to a man involves the same kind of commitment as
our marriage to God. Just as we can't be halfway
Christians we also can't be halfway married. It's
a very great commitment and responsibility. It ties
you to that man—chains of love.*

The above excerpts constitute a touching tribute to her parents; without even realizing it, she had deeply internalized the
value structures of both. She had learned by *example* from those
she loved most on this earth. If she had lived and married, her
marriage doubtless would have reflected the Christian marriage
of her parents.

Cris was also very close to her two brothers with whom she
spent many hours discussing personal, religious and philosophi-
cal questions.

Cris was about one year younger than her older brother. As
children, they were constant playmates. Early in life, at each new
adventure, such as starting school, it was her brother who guided
and protected her. As they grew older their relationship changed

somewhat; this stage of her life in which her older brother was her guide and protector made a lasting impact upon her. She stated many years later in her musical composition, *He Turned on the Light*:

> And I was very frightened and stood very still.
> The darkness crept upon me and gave me a chill.
> And then my brother he came and he lit a match
>   for me.
> And I was so happy cause I could see.

Cris and her older brother *shared* their joys, hopes, and fears, and sought each *other's* advice on personal problems.

Cris' relationship to her younger brother was equally close but somewhat different. Being five years older, it was Cris who was the guide, the teacher, and the protector. Their relationship was strengthened by a common talent for music. As a child, Cris enjoyed playing school; she was the teacher and her brother the student. The subject Cris stressed was music, with emphasis on singing and playing the violin.

From early childhood Cris and her maternal grandmother were joined by a strong spiritual bond, a bond that could not be broken by death itself. Her grandmother, a pianist, and Cris spent many joyful hours singing and playing the violin and piano together. Her grandmother preceded Cris in death by about six months. One of her last requests was that Cris sing at her funeral. This Cris did with a happy sadness. That evening, following the funeral, Cris wrote:

> *Sang at Grandma's funeral—felt her singing*
> *along in a chorus of heavenly joy.*

As she had special people so she also had a special place in her life, a place where she could *escape* from people. The family owned a cabin at a lake in northern Minnesota where they spent many hours together during the warmer months of the year. Cris loved the lake, the woods, the closeness to nature afforded by visits to this summer home. She continued to spend time there with the family until the very end. She had a favorite spot in the woods which she often visited alone to communicate with nature and with God. She named this spot the "Isle of Pines." I visited this place after her death and it reminded me of a miniature cathedral designed by God. It consists of a small, grassy clearing rimmed by towering pines. The only sounds one hears are sounds of nature and the hum of the wind in the pines. Standing there, I could almost feel her presence, sitting beneath the pines, dreaming beautiful dreams, thinking inspiring thoughts.

Like Jesus, Cris had a very special place in her heart for children. She loved children and received more satisfaction in relating with them than she did in relating with adults. If her life had been spared, she would probably have brought her love for Jesus, as well as her love for and her talent in music, to serve the spiritual needs of children. Working with children would have given her a great deal of satisfaction. Having received pressure from a number of sources to devote her life exclusively to music, she at one time threatened to throw her violin into the river! Music for music's sake was insufficient. Music as a means of serving God and man was the only acceptable way—and her service probably would have been primarily to children. A number of her writings verify this. In letters to a friend, one on 7/30/72, the second on 8/10/72, she writes:

> *I love children. My aunt has a little girl about*
> *three years old. I had so much fun with her. To*
> *children everything is a wonder, unique. They let*

their imaginations run loose. It's so fresh. I find it much easier to talk to kids than to adults. There's no put-on with kids.

And in the second letter referring to the children in the junior choir which she directed, she stated:

I've got a lot to tell you about the things I've learned from my kids at church. Too much for a letter. We'll have to talk about it. One can learn much from children. They're very honest about love.

Two entries in her diary, one dated 11/23/72, the second dated 1/6/73, reinforce these statements. In the first entry she says:

I love children! I see it more every day. The freshness and exuberance some of us older ones have lost.

And the later entry:

Children are so special. Not sweet or darling, but something much greater, fresh and honest.

So it was in children that Cris was finding what she was unable to find in adults. And it was with children that, had she lived, she would have been best able to serve her Lord.

Cris—God

$\mathcal{N}$ow let us look more closely at Cris' relationship with God as revealed primarily by her writings. Her parents relate that from childhood she was Christ oriented and that she had never gone through any noticeable periods of question and doubt. Even in college when the faith of many young people is challenged by "wise" professors, by books, and by learning, Cris' faith remained unshaken. In a diary entry dated 12/8/72 she stated:

> *Books—years of learning and exploring, and ideas—often much garbage. All is vanity. I hold by a magical thread only to God.*

This, in her freshman year in college!

Nevertheless, a struggle for light did prevail in the first sixteen years of her life. She was beset by fears and was convinced at times that a monster within her was battling for her soul. She makes reference to this fear twice, once in a high school essay and later in one of her early musical compositions. In her high school paper she wrote:

> *There is a monster inside of me. I'm sure of it now. For a long time I wondered if it was really there, wondered if it was only a part of my imagination, only a tool which I used to torture myself. But now I am sure it is there for even in my imagination— it is real.... It lives in a cave of darkness within me.... Oh, the horrors I can imagine to be there.... I do not want to be a part of the darkness and empty dampness of the cave. I want to live where it is light and where sun shines and where I can run in the wind.*

And from her musical composition *He Turned On The Light*:

> *And then once there came a night that when I went to bed I needed a light shining up above my head. And the darkness was lonely and I dreamed awful dreams. And the monster that came made me toss and scream.*

But with the help of God she conquered the darkness and the monster within her, and in an undated diary entry she stated:

> *Now it is clear to me. No more darkness. No more loneliness. I want Jesus. I want to be with Him and in Him and He in me. Now I am no longer afraid of that dark world. It has no power.*

This early period of darkness in her life, as she struggled to make full personal contact with Jesus and the light, left a deep scar on her sensitive nature. Even after she had conquered it and walked in the light she still made reference to it. In a touching musical composition, *Life on a Swing*, written when she was sixteen, she developed the theme that life without Christ is a nothing life that goes nowhere; and she concluded by telling those who have not yet found Jesus to fall on their knees and say, "Here's my hand, will You lead me to Your light?" And in the poignant melody, *He Turned on The Light*, she concludes with the lines:

> *And then my Jesus came and He shone His light*
> *for me. And I am so happy cause I can see.*

From the written evidence, one can conclude that at about age sixteen Cris was victorious in her struggle with the powers of darkness and that she walked thereafter in the brilliant light of Jesus. From that point until her death, her relationship with God became increasingly more personal. From then until the end she was in constant communion with God. From Him she drew the strength needed to maintain a rigorous schedule and still find time to help others. "*Last night we talked,*" she stated, "*and today is new and fresh.*" This relationship with Jesus became so intimate and so personal that the "marriage to Christ" concept became very real to her. In an undated diary entry she states:

> *I am married to the Lord—Him I will follow or*
> *only death can result as the emptiness of a wife*
> *removed from her husband.*

In a letter to a friend Cris said happily:

> *I'm Jesus' bride—Wow, what a joyous thing!*

A high emotional period followed. Cris was ecstatic about this newfound relationship with Christ. It seems that she had finally found the love that had so long eluded her. She had now found fulfillment. A number of diary entries illustrate this but the following single entry dated 12/22/72 will suffice:

> *Jesus holds me. Oh, how I love Him! My heart sings now. I fly with Him soaring above the mountains. He is what matters.... I rejoice. He is my all.*

This intimate relationship with God did not diminish or level off in the ensuing months as one would normally expect. If anything, it became stronger, closer, more constant, more mature. On 3/24/73 she recorded:

> *My touch with God has changed. He is in all my life—not separate. He is my always prayer, not just my special one. He is my whole life, one continuous embrace, not scattered moments of ecstasy.*

As one studies her writings, one cannot help but notice a number of references which indicate personal *physical* contact with God. Below are some examples from her diary:

> *The hand has touched me. Now that it has it can never go away.*

> *Today on the ocean, I met Christ and was filled with Him and loved Him and we walked and joined.*

Jesus holds *me*.

I've seen God and touched *His hand*.

On reading this, one is tempted to conclude that these contacts were imaginative and figurative, not literal. But an event related by Cris' parents which occurred approximately three years before her death makes one wonder. One Sunday afternoon, Cris came down from her room. She asked her parents if either of them had been in her room while she was resting. They had not. She insisted that they must have been. When her father inquired about the reason for her question she said that while she was resting someone had entered her room and had placed a hand softly on the top of her head. This event was dismissed as a dream or as a figment of her imagination. After her death, when her diary was discovered, however, some serious doubts were raised. Perhaps she *had* been touched by the hand of God that afternoon. If so, for what reasons? To assure her personally of His love? We don't know, we can only speculate; for now, "We see through a glass darkly."

The years of her growth in Christ were accompanied by a strange feeling of expectation; she felt that she was moving slowly toward an inevitable something which she was unable or unwilling to describe. This period of expectation or waiting covered about one year in her life and apparently terminated ten months before her death. Following is documentation of this "waiting period" which begins with a feeling of foreboding but ends with a feeling of joy:

12/3/72
Death, I wait for it to come. I'm so tired of waiting. Waiting for what? Not death. Be patient. Rest and wait.

12/4/72

I worry about time, for I have to wait, and I don't know what I am waiting for.

1/6/73

As I wait, that thing which I wait for grows further and further away. What shall I do? Should I sit and wait for it or should I follow and fight for it? Follow? But I don't even know what it is.

1/24/73

I grow so tired of the waiting that my body aches with it, but it is God's will and a part of the plan. I try and forget, but it is always there, buried inside.

3/24/73

The waiting has changed. It is there, but so deep I cannot feel it, cannot know of its existence, but God knows and cares for it.

5/9/73

The rains came this morning and touched me softly. Waiting is almost done, and tomorrow flowers will bloom. The winter is past and much has died. The rain clears away the garbage and heals the wounds. I live for the rains and today, for tomorrow will come, and I want to be ready.

11/7/73

It is good and happy to long and to wait and rest.
It is right, my waiting has changed.

12/31/73

All my waiting is over and yet I wait completely
different. There is no longing, no pain, no confu-
sion, only peace and willingness.

It is impossible to know what Cris had in mind when she penned the entry above dated May 9, 1973. We can only speculate. If it had been written within another context at another point in time it could be accepted as only a beautiful poetic expression. But read within the context of "waiting" it could very well be symbolic and consequently subject to interpretation. Certainly many interpretations are possible. I offer the following. She says, *"The rains came this morning and touched me softly."* We know from her writings and songs that to Cris rain was a symbol of God's love.

"Waiting is almost done and tomorrow flowers will bloom..." describe death, the beauty of heaven, and union with Christ as opposed to the "winter" sterility and "garbage" ugliness and decay which typify life on earth. *"Tomorrow will come, and I want to be ready..."* expresses a wish to be prepared with "oil for her lamp," as were the wise virgins in the Biblical parable.

So the final months of her life were spent in hard work as usual but also in casting out all the non-essentials in her relationship with Christ—so that she might meet Him finally free and unencumbered. A letter to a friend written five days before her death shows that she had succeeded in doing this:

All the words and studies and philosophies and rules of religion don't make sense to me anymore. It's just that I love Jesus and He loves me—that simple—and if that love exists, everything naturally follows. You talked about the gift of prophecy. Somehow, that is the same way, just not important to me anymore. I know God—I don't have to wait for prophecy to hear His words—He always speaks to me.

It's strange, so much has changed—so much quieter, so much more of an even flow. It's good!

Two final incidents need to be mentioned before this brief introduction to Cris is brought to a close:

Approximately one month prior to her death, Cris had been visited, while at work, by a young woman who had been a very close friend in high school. This young woman was attending college in another town so they hadn't seen each other for quite some time. The two girls arranged to bike later in the day to a local cemetery to talk, the very cemetery in which Cris was to be buried one month later. The young women sat on a hill overlooking the spot where Cris' body is now buried. In themselves, these were strange happenings, but even stranger was the feeling shared by both girls that this would be the last time they would ever meet—a feeling that proved to be prophetic!

The final incident involves the circumstances of her death. The car in which she was a passenger was struck broadside by a semi-trucktrailer. The car was totally demolished. Cris was virtually unmarked! She had died instantly from a broken neck. It seemed as if God had said, "The waiting is over. I want her with me now—but I want to spare her the pain and suffering which often accompany death."

So ends the sad yet inspiring story of Cris, a young woman who sought and found the kind of union with God that most of us don't even dare dream of—a union which brought her the peace and happiness that pass all human understanding. She was aptly described by St. Paul in a letter to the Christians at Corinth many years ago:

> By pureness, by knowledge, by long-suffering,
> by kindness, by the Holy Ghost, by love unfeigned.
> As unknown, and yet well known;
> As sorrowful, yet always rejoicing.

Blessed are the pure in heart:
for they shall see God.

Jesus of Nazareth

Cristine's
Notes and Journal

Top: Cris and her brother in her home in Austin, Minnesota (about age six). Bottom: Cris with parents and brothers in student housing, Syracuse University (about age 8).

Top: Cris on Oregon coast (about age 5). Bottom: Cris on North Carolina Coast (age 7).

November 20, 1971

*T*oday was a day of memories. Memories are strange things, for you know they are a part of you and you know they affect you, but they can never be relived or refelt the same way they were before. There is no turning back in time. Once you have experienced something there is no way of emptying it from the container that is you.

I was at a fine concert tonight and, while I was there, there were many thoughts and emotions going through me. I'm not sure now what they were, but I know that I learned much while sitting there. Also, there was a temptation to go back to the old way of life—and then, of course, I know there is no turning back.

A thought I discovered today: one who searches may find a vast emptiness, but that emptiness can be filled; one who never searches will never find emptiness and will never be full.

I have a wish to write things down so that they may be saved and shared. However, I'm not very good at saying what I mean—I want to learn, to stop lying. First I must stop lying to myself. It is not as great a sin to lie to others as it is to lie to yourself. I don't want to live in unreality and lies. *Lord help me to face myself*—we must always question for only then will we find answers—there are many contradictions and conflicts inside of me—they must be burned away and made pure by a child-like faith. I must learn to accept all things as important. If you feel that many things are trivial, pretty soon all things are trivial and then you end up with nothing. Yes, all is important because *all* is a part of life and life is important!

The artificial in me must fall away and I must no longer pretend. All the hidden fears and dark spots must be uncovered and turned to light. I must slowly be brought from my distant spot and learn to love and share with others—any form of communication in which I am asked to let part of my inner self be seen is very frightening to me. This fear must be conquered through the perfect love of God.

I have so long lived in the unreal world that I can no longer enjoy or see beauty in much reality. I have for so long dwelt in sorrow that I have forgotten how to have fun. I must learn this. I have for so long lived in the tension of endless searching and trying to grasp a spring that always breaks that I am no longer able to relax and live in peace. I must learn this. For so long I have seen only hell in the present that I always lived rather in the future with its false dreams. I am no longer able to turn my eyes to "now" and let the tomorrow take care of itself. I must learn this. I have tried to understand and comprehend life with my own tiny wisdom and only became lost. Now I must learn to be as a child and there I will find the simplicity of truth in Jesus Christ.

For many years I have been afraid to look in the mirror; when I did, I found ugliness, fear, and vast emptiness. When Jesus came, I hid many of these things away and thought that in Jesus I could run away from them. He made me stop, see each one and face it with His strength and power. I must learn much and He will teach me much.

Now I am facing the greatest thing of all—my fear of love—for love is both the greatest of pain and the greatest of joy. He is teaching me to overcome my greatest fear. I have searched only a little in a vast amount, but already can see the beauty overflowing of this great gift. Only as a little child can these things be learned; only with eyes on Jesus can they be seen clearly and without confusion.

> *Jesus, make me as a little child and help me keep my eyes on You. When I get scared, take me up and comfort me and continue to teach me out of Your precious cup of life and infinity.*

⌘ ⌘ ⌘ ⌘

Why may something be set down on paper? Can lead and plant fibers depict an idea?

Does this world live in everyone or have I been somewhere and seen something no one else can see. I'm going back to that place again. Why? Did I ever really escape from it? I'm alone in this crowd of people. Why? I could make myself fit in. Why don't I? Do I like loneliness and depression? If I like it, then I should stay there. Yet, why do I want Jesus' light? Do I really? I've seen it now. I've seen a glimpse of it and begun to let it into my world.

Now I'm half way between two places. Which one to take? Which one holds true happiness? What is true happiness? Am I happy when I'm sad? I seem to like darkness and loneliness. Is happiness possible? Is it something that should be looked for? Everybody could go where I am couldn't they? Why don't they? Are they afraid? Are they truly happy? No question can ever be answered positively. Everything is part of an infinite web, a web in which the parts do not work together to form the structure, but continually fight each other and strangle each other. What are we all searching for? Is there anything worth finding?

There must be a God—there must be something greater and beyond all this. I've seen God and touched His hand. Why did He let me see Him? Why did He let me into His world for a second? Why does He beckon me to come in? Does He want loneliness? No! He must want a friend. How can He love me? How can He ask me in? Why is it so easy for Him to offer His world and so hard for me to open mine?

Come in Jesus!

He's making me let Him come in. Only God has the power to do this.

Jesus help! This battle in me has to be conquered! I have to learn to share—to take—to give—to love—to be happy. Teach me Jesus—please, I need Your help—only You have a great enough understanding. Turn Your eyes to me for only a second of a second. I know I'm not worth any fraction, no matter how small, of that time. How can You want to bother with me? How can You love me even enough to turn Your eyes to me for even a second much less die for me? I can't see why You should care at all. Why do You? If You didn't, I wouldn't be fighting You now. Why is it so hard for me to accept love? Teach me how. Teach me how to give love. Why do You bother to try to teach such a dumb student? I'm a baby who's even too dumb to know how to drink milk (all babies except me know that by nature). Why don't You just let me starve? Why do You keep washing me in the milk of Your love? Why? Where am I? What is real?

⸎ ⸎ ⸎ ⸎

The words begin to flow and there is sun outside. My mind spins in a thousand rhythms and there is dew on my heart, sweating in the fragrance of spring. Time passes and as I sit and watch it travel by me, I grow sleepy. People enter the scene, play their part and then disappear, but I remain. My hand grows tired from reaching out and I wish that one, only one, would stop with time and pull me onto the road. Sleepy as at a tennis game. I must rest. I must turn my eyes to the other side, but cannot.

The pastor speaks, and I know his words are pointed to me, but I cannot cry. Will anyone listen anyway? The things that I know I want grow further away and I continue where it doesn't matter. They look at me and say that I am intelligent and have a bright future. Not without the pain and the sweat, that they don't see.

⸎ ⸎ ⸎ ⸎

Since the person spoke to me, I am different. How? I know, I need and I run. I run from need. It is such pain. Turn away—it's easier to follow the lighted normal way.

The hand has touched me. Now that it has, it can never go away. It remains, a part of me. I try to forget. I cannot. It has happened; it exists. There is truly no turning back. It has changed me and I cannot pretend it hasn't.

When all is so brilliantly colored that it hurts the eye, after a time all its brilliance turns into a grey sheet.

I am separated and can no longer touch them. I feel as if I am so far off that they all look at me and wonder. I have seen the questioning stares. I try, but cannot conform. Too stubborn, too decided. I know that I am not easy to get along with. I say what I think. Sometimes I know it happens. What to do? I don't know. Can I, should I change?

How many times does one find a precious jewel in one's life. Once? Maybe twice? Maybe never? Once one has seen it, what happens? One cannot forget.

To say, or to act? Words mean nothing unless they are filled by action. The act is truth.

To die…to rest…peace. To be as a tree which can rest for a season and then come back to life—this I wish for. But one cannot die and then return; one must continue on.

My day is filled with the trivial and I am glad for it keeps the thought from creeping up on me. Where have I gone? I am afraid to think. I am afraid of hope for I have seen hope knocked down too many times. My arms are tired from trying to rebuild. No more hope. Without hope, nothing falls—but all is grey.

৵৽ ৵৽ ৵৽ ৵৽

What is God? The question that has always disturbed mankind—the question that all men must ask themselves sometime in life—the question that deepens the chasm of the mind beyond the wildest imagination. It is the utmost of complexity with its endless dimensions and new ideas—yet at the same time the utmost of simplicity—the most basic question of mankind. It lives in every human soul and must be faced in order to be answered.

Hate, anger, jealousy, prudence, selfishness, emptiness, longing, suffering, sorrow, weakness, struggling, sinking, despair, tears, tired, weary, confusion, nothing, fear, barriers, walls, lonely, wary, worry, restless, tides, searching, wanting, sarcasm, frown, hope, joy, peace, love, light, radiance, color, simplicity, freshness, fulfillment, love, joy, laughter, faith, hope, strength, security, rest, achievement, freedom, expansion, fullness, richness, love, peace, truth, friends, steady, goodness, mercy, forgiveness, grace, love, letters, messages, love, sharing, learning, loving, giving, asking and finding, forgetting, rebirth, children, honesty, love, unity, friends, together, helping, receiving, love—the greatest of these is love.

What is and what is not? Where is reality? What am I? Who am I? Am I alone? Am I part of all? What is the inner world? Where is escape? Why is all? Confusion? Who cares? What is love? What are words? What can be communicated? Is there more beyond? Beyond what? Is it all many worlds or one big world? What is freedom? Where is freedom? Who is free? Why must we be held in chains of our own making? Does everyone see? Why are some blind? What is the difference between dark and light, bad and good? Why is all so infinite, so incomprehensible? Why is it hard for me to spell things right? Why do people smoke? Why do they try to run away? Why is looking in the mirror so scary? Why does God love us? Why did He create us? Why does rain fall from the sky? What is the extent of the universe? Does it terminate? What is the extent of God? What is eternity? What are the things of the world? Why do they fall away at the hope of something greater? What is nature? What is real? What is touch? What is life? What is death? Where is warmth? What is love? Where is love? Who is love? What is a place? What is existence? Does existence exist?

Simplicity and answers lie only in Jesus Christ—the chasm of endless questions is filled with answers to the unanswerable.

ࠬ ࠬ ࠬ ࠬ

It's all so official, so plastic. Number—a card—a form—a face. Facts and systems pour out. And what is their purpose? What is real learning? It is nothing—to be forgotten—stashed away in files of the mind to grow dusty, never to be used again. —All for the sake of a title. A label to show that it is there— even though it is never used and is of no value. We label according to that which is worthless. Where is the real person, inner, the soul? Yet they affect. But, am I the total of my facts, or am I me? I want to be me—they don't allow it. Why they? They want the same as I; however, they are afraid to admit it. I want to learn. But not for the sake of a label, only for the sake of learning. It is what it is. Nothing else.

❧ ❧ ❧ ❧

I want you to be you. Change, but be you. Don't be what they want you to be. Don't be what I might want you to be. Be you. I may not like you for you—fine. I am me. I cannot pretend. But you, don't you pretend to be different so that I will like you, or I won't. Be you.

❧ ❧ ❧ ❧

They set it up. But who are they? No different. They know no more of what is right than I do. Let them. Only I don't have to follow. I can decide for myself. I can do what I want.

❧ ❧ ❧ ❧

If it would never have happened. They say it's better this way. It's not. Because I know—

❧ ❧ ❧ ❧

Alone…Yes, but always alone in the end. It's OK. I don't mind. There is life. These are people. There are facts. We are all alone in the end. The facts separate, become individual, smaller

64

and smaller. They are more precious. Journey through the mass till you see each separate fact. There you also have seen nothing.

There is a difference. Those of us who know try to hide it away—try to become a part of the unseeing mass. We cannot. We know ourselves—we know each other—and we know the mass. It is no use.

"I" and "they" at the same time. Where am I going? I know what I need and yet walk away from it—in favor of what "they" want. I'm tired!

Sometimes it happens—and you wish it never had—because you know—you've seen. And you can never go back. You want to—you try—but it's a part of you. You've seen, felt, and cannot unsee or unfeel—and you know how hopeless it is.

❧❧ ❧❧ ❧❧ ❧❧

Now it is clear to me. No more darkness. No more loneliness. I know what I want. I want Jesus. I want to be with Him and in Him and He in me. Now I am no longer afraid of that dark world. It has no power over me. Jesus loves me. I want to serve Him and to love and share. I want to live in simplicity and joy. That is my hope. Now I must learn. Many trials come. I can see them ahead. I'm not afraid—Jesus cares for me.

❧❧ ❧❧ ❧❧ ❧❧

Windows fascinate me. I can look through to the world outside. Yet, I am separated. I can lie back and rest while the outside goes madly by. The pain comes when, sooner or later, I have to go and join.

The next time or the past—go! I'm tired. Let me live for now. I tell them of the pain. They laugh or don't understand. They have no part—it's OK. I have done it to me. It's OK.

It exists. No blame. Everything or nothing. We are so tiny, so narrow. Why do we see so little? Because to see too much hurts, causes indecision and confusion. People.

If the outside is hard enough, they will never see the inside. They may wonder, but they will never explore for they are afraid of what they may find.

When one has seen both the light and the darkness, then one truly knows brilliance.

∽◦◦ ∽◦◦ ∽◦◦ ∽◦◦

The sweet smell of rotting leaves and soft rains. Solid moist earth—cool to touch. Soft petals of a wild rose. A wind speaking in the branches of the trees—here is God.

∽◦◦ ∽◦◦ ∽◦◦ ∽◦◦

When I stop and rest from the hurry and bustle of today's world, I can see—see much further and much deeper. I can see before me the whole total concept of life in all its complexity and in all its simplicity. Many times my vision is focused on one certain concept or image, but at the same time all else that I have discovered awaits in the shadows and all that I haven't discovered stretches before me. In certain moments I see things in my heart and my soul that words can never express. How can I share them?

All men are tied together by a certain bond. We must discover it and develop it and bring it out so that man may live together in peace, not in turmoil. I think I now know what the bond is—it is God! God lives deep inside of all men.

The problem lies in that men don't turn to God. They bury him under all the worldly and superficial. The way to find God is by questioning yourself and being totally honest with yourself. The greatest sin is lying to yourself. You must question in order to create a chasm of emptiness for God to fill—then turn your eyes to Jesus Christ and know that He loves you and you are so precious to Him that He died for you and weeps for you when you turn the wrong way. He only wants to give you of

His wonderful light to fill your cup of emptiness. He only wants to give; just ask, seek and knock and He will answer, and fear and darkness will be gone and locked away forever.

∽∽∽ ∽∽∽ ∽∽∽ ∽∽∽

When the rich man asked Jesus which was the greatest commandment, Jesus said simply, "love God and love man." All things done in love are good and all things not done in love are wrong. Love is the final test. Deep and honest love can only be given by God. It is the gift He gives us when we look on Him. The only way to obtain it is through faith. All other rules and commandments that we set up are totally worthless. We must have a simple childlike faith and through that we will receive love and after love will come the good works that He wishes for us. Anything done out of jealousy, pride or selfishness— anything other than love is wrong no matter what strict rules we follow. And love is obtained by faith in Him who loves us.

∽∽∽ ∽∽∽ ∽∽∽ ∽∽∽

The eyes of man—golden sunshine— ripened fields—the miracle of life—Nature has many faces, many moods—all of them say something different; all of them live deep within the heart of man for man is part of the earth.

Soil, rich and earthy, moist from freshly fallen rain—it is cool to the touch. There is a stability about soil, a basicness, a quality that grips and holds us solid—"And God formed man of the dust of the ground"—It is a part of us and we a part of it—our rock, our basis, our foundation.

Rain—washes over us—warm cleansing rain, hard driving rain—slow drizzle. Rain comes together and forms into a life-line—a river carrying away wrong and worn—bringing fresh-ness and newness—Rain. We cannot live without it to cleanse our wounds and allow us to live again.

❧❧ ❧❧ ❧❧ ❧❧

Words must fall away and we must learn to feel and love with our hearts instead of our lips. Love must be centered outwardly instead of inwardly—it must be a pure and unselfish love for others. Only this will save mankind and this is a gift that only God can give. It is the gift of a faith in Jesus Christ.

❧❧ ❧❧ ❧❧ ❧❧

Personal thoughts on myself—

I have been searching for myself, and what I really want to be. In my search I have visited many different worlds and have seen many things. They have become a part of me and I a part of them.

I have visited the quietness of nature and felt the joy of sitting alone in the woods in the morning listening to the birds singing and the dew dripping from the trees. And I have felt love for this deep inside and I have seen God here—and I have become a part of it and it has come onto me.

I have also been to the world of cement and bricks—buildings, slums, and cars. I have seen a strange beauty there and have grown to love it also. There stands the majesty of what man has done with what God has given him. Here are many mistakes, failures and successes. That which has failed must be loved also and must be learned from and attempted again. This place I have also learned to love for it is a part of God and I have become a part of it and it a part of me.

I have entered a world of freedom—the freedom that some of the hippie ideals have tried to achieve. This is how some in my generation have reached out for it. Many have failed and only become tied up in greater prisons. However, it is not only of my generation. Man has reached out for this freedom since the beginning of time. I have seen it and felt it and it has touched me. And I have felt free, running through the wind and no one can take that freedom away for it is in me where no one but God can touch.

I have also become imprisoned within many things during my life for Satan is constantly setting up things for me to try to escape into so that he can trap me. I have fallen into his traps many times. I have seen the darkness there and have felt his claws digging into me. It is a prison of utter hopelessness, darkness, and nothing—and it has become a part of me and I can never escape—even through God—the knowledge of it or the memory of it.

I have been to the world of the intellectual—a world of books, writing, complication, and not many answers but many questions. This has helped me much by showing me many things to search for and many things to want. However, I was not able to find the answers and it has hurt me by giving me a feeling of nothingness and hopelessness. It has taken away all the natural securities and left only a sea—continuously stirring—constantly restless.

Yet, I have also seen the world of the simple, the accepting, the childlike. I have felt the warmth of crying in someone's arms and being told that it will be all right. I have felt the security of knowing that someone cares even though they can't understand. In God I have felt the security of knowing that I am never alone. And both the sea and the peace exist in me and are constantly fighting each other for a throne in my life.

And I have seen the world of the good—the pure, the white—what is considered holy. A world where people suffer, for they deny themselves many beautiful things. Yet where they feel purity and piety. I have seen here many who are good and have much love. Also many who are hypocrites. There is also a world of what is considered bad and ugly that I have been to— and here I have seen many who have suffered and lost and many who are hypocrites. But I have also seen much love here—not a love of duty, but a love of kinship. In both places, many are loyal and good, but there are also many who are merely fooling themselves. Both I have seen and they exist in me and I can see from one into another and they contradict. Yet, God is in both and both are in me.

I have also been to a world of culture and refinement—formals, opera, and art galleries. I have found in this great beauty and great depth; yet, much that is useless because of the way in which people use it. But it is deep inside me and I have seen God in it.

I have been to a world of mysticism, fantasy and that which goes beyond words—and I have seen much of God here and it all lives inside me like a cavern of constantly changing waves of color. But it is not as the sea, for the floor is solid.

I have also seen the world of reality and that which can only be touched, tasted, seen, heard, or smelled. This world is also a part of God and a part of me.

I have been to all these places and many more—and I have found in all of them—beauty and ugliness and God and Satan. And they are all a part of me and my insides are in a turmoil because they are all there fighting one another and contradicting one another. And the biggest contradiction is that it is all separate and opposite, but all one—all restless, but all peaceful—all useless—but all valuable and precious. It is all complicated and all simple—

I have seen all these places but have never been able to settle into one as most people can. They have all become a part of me and I of them. Yet, none are really me for I am all of them. I am a misfit!

Before God, they were all separate—now they are all united. Before God, they were all complicated—now they are simple. Yet, because I am imperfect and human, they are still very separate and restless. God is showing me each one and I am becoming a part of each. I no longer have to hide any of these places away in order to keep my eyes on God—for Satan has used these places much and made them ugly. Now they are being made open and united and they are becoming me, and I them and in them, God, and in me, God.

⸎ ⸎ ⸎ ⸎

Why do we have to ask questions we would rather not have answered? Why do we want to have things that bring up pain?

What is crazy? A swirling, whirling mass of logic. What is normal? A swirling, whirling mass of nonsense.

We are drawn to fear. Overcome. Bravery is fear. Where is security?

What is happiness? Why do we want it? Is there not joy in sorrow? Love in sorrow? Peace in sorrow? Good in sorrow?

Food. We must eat or we die. Yet, we die even though we eat. Food is different yet all the same.

A rainbow—a promise—hope.

Rain—love.

I am asked to carry that which I cannot bear. Or am I asked to ask for help carrying that which I cannot bear?

People—so many people. Crowds. Alive—yet each one is a dead face.

I read books of things that happened long ago. And wonder—Why they mean so much to me.

The river.

Now I really know nothing…. Yet I think I know a lot. Hands reaching out—grasping. For what?—that is the question.

Yet, in my nothingness I am happy. I am peaceful. Before, I was afraid. What has changed in my nothingness to make it so?

⸎ ⸎ ⸎ ⸎

Why today? Why not tomorrow, yesterday, a year ago? What is so special about today?

Fall—it was supposed to snow today. It didn't. It was supposed to snow every day for the past week. It didn't.

It is a day of floating. I must concentrate on Biology, the stages of mitosis and meiosis. If I let my mind wander, it becomes confused. Better to fill it with facts.

I don't understand people, or friendships. Friends when they need me, gone when they don't. Grasping on for a companion; gone, proud, and independent the next day.

I don't understand love. Why? There are no reasons. You can't love someone for a reason or not love for a reason. You either love or you don't. A gift.

Black and white—so simple. Too bad most is grey.

My dream of fall—to be a tree. To die and to sink into the ground for rest until spring. Rest soul.

⌘ ⌘ ⌘ ⌘

My trust is in God. There is nowhere else to put my trust. Friends fail, people fail, I fail, but God never fails.

He knows me better than I know me. He knows what is best for me, and will bring it to pass. I am a leaf floating, resting, in the river of His love.

If something is weak on the outside, the weak parts are slowly scraped away to reveal the strength of the center. However, if something is strong on the outside and weak on the inside, the inside only grows weaker and weaker as it remains. The outside must grow harder and harder to cover the weakness of the inside. They quench my thirst.—Many waters cannot quench love.

⌘ ⌘ ⌘ ⌘

Why am I in the middle? Two worlds—not completely a part of one, not completely a part of the other. I desperately want to choose, to commit myself to one, but I cannot. I cannot live without either, and I cannot live in the middle.

> Two roads
>   They separate
> I cannot travel both.

രജ്ക രജ്ക രജ്ക രജ്ക

> He is pure—I have ulterior motives
> He is a child—I am complex
> He is concerned—I am selfish
> He is polite—I am rude
> He speaks—I walk away
> He is a rock—I am a body of water

രജ്ക രജ്ക രജ്ക രജ്ക

I am one of them. They are marked. Nothing changes. They may be good or they may be bad. Yet, they are the same.

They are different, set apart. They seek after the world of light, cherries, and lace. But no...only darkness, loneliness.

They see God, know His love—love God, but cannot find the light. The darkness pulls and grasps. There is no escaping. Hell is a memory, a part. Light is a memory, a part. Wanting light, knowing it, seeing it, reaching it, feeling, not to remain. They are marked. I am marked.

They stand in a circle, laughing, gossiping. They share their secrets, joys and sorrows, loves. Their eyes are bright and teeth white. They put on just the right amount of make-up and their nylons never have runs. Fingers with nail polish. I go to them. They open their arms. I laugh. I gossip. I wear just the right amount of make-up, nail polish, no runs. I watch me, and I hold that which is precious outside the circle. I don't want it eaten up. I hide it deep within my heart.

❧ ❧ ❧ ❧

To watch them eat gives me peace. I don't taste, but give my love to their taste. Many hours just to watch their big clumsy hands. Time to see them lean back and sigh; they go away to read while I clean up. I give them my love.

❧ ❧ ❧ ❧

He said, "Let us rest our eyes
    on each other's eyes."
He told me to stop drawing those lines on them.
    I never wore them again.
He told me to sing for him.
    I wrote him a song.
He told me to give him my hand.
    I gave him my hand.
He told me to think of him.
    He was there even in my dreams.
He told me to stop loving him.
    I cannot.

❧ ❧ ❧ ❧

I am sick.
I cannot be.
They need me:
    Wash their dishes
    Heat their chili
    Pick up their dirty clothes
I get up.

❧ ❧ ❧ ❧

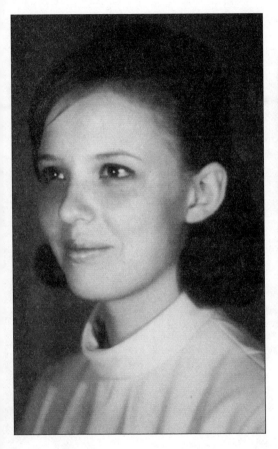

Left: Cris in a home portrait, age 17.
Above: Cris at the Isle of Pines, age 14.

Left: Cris in a home portrait, age 20..
Below: Cris as a teenager talking to her friend.
Bottom left: The Messengers—Cris is second from the left, front row, age 16.

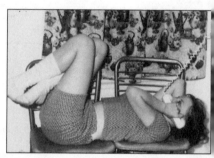

He calls.
I am not free for two weeks.
He is sad.
I cry.
    It snows.

             ᐩ   ᐩ   ᐩ   ᐩ

Last night it snowed. Our first snow. I must go for a walk today. I remember the first snow of last year—how special it was. 1971. It is special this year too. In a different way. I don't know why.

Today I must vote for the president of the United States.

             ᐩ   ᐩ   ᐩ   ᐩ

"Talent" has been on my mind. To be one of the fortunate who has been blessed with talent. What curse is greater? One must always give. One must sacrifice that which he wants to do in order to do that which he can do and no one else can do.

I am a violinist—I *must* use the talent. God has given me the gift that most don't have. I am needed.

I sing. I must use it. God has given me a special gift. I am needed.

I am brilliant. I must use it. The world needs doctors, explorers, thinkers. I am needed.

I can teach. I must use it. Not many can teach well. The system needs help. I am needed.

I can listen. My friends need to rest their head on someone's shoulder—to put their burdens. I am needed.

My mother works. She does not have time to cook or do the dishes. I will fit it in. I am needed.

A boy calls. He is shy, wants to take me out. He needs a girl—not me; but me to learn the courage. I go. He is at ease. He learns and moves on. I am needed.

What do I want? I don't know. It's been lost in the confusion. No one allows me to look. I am needed.

Who will play for me?
Who will sing for me?
Who will teach me?
Upon whose shoulder can I cry?
Who will listen to me?
Who will love me?
I AM NEEDED!

❧ ❧ ❧ ❧

Kids did a beautiful job of singing in Sunday School. I'm really proud of them. They shine. I've learned a lot from them and they a lot from me.

Sundays are lonely. Sometimes everything springs up into nothingness. Other times all is very intense. I see a brilliant light and a deep darkness.

Things too precious to be shared with anyone. Yet, so precious that they must be shared with someone.

I have begun to learn to share God in other ways. I'm not a hard core witnesser. Letting Him shine is more important than a lot of words. I hope He does shine. I want Him to. Above all else, I want to be His.

❧ ❧ ❧ ❧

Strangeness—this strange relationship with God. I love Him much. I can trust only Him, not things. It's harder that way.

I get along; yet, I am alone. There is a certain arrogance, stubbornness. They don't understand. They stand afar and are afraid to come close. I don't encourage them. They don't know their feelings: admiration or hatred. I can lie to them and care not whether they believe. I need one stronger, one who knows what is true or untrue, one who draws close with powers. I wait.

My words, as my heart, do not tell the complete story. Parts I have hidden away. I cannot face the pain of knowing. Yet, they are there—deep within. I only can pray.

Ruth said: "Whither thou goest, I will go." I do not. I say, "Whither I wishest to go, I will go." Yet, I want to be the other, and cannot.

Friends, ah how strange. Why do they make no difference to me? I make friends easily—laugh—gossip. Yet, they don't matter. I cannot trust them in the end. They fall away. They don't understand. Only God remains.

I cannot say those things. Only in spirit can they pass from one to another. Only in my eyes, my heart. No one sees; no one feels.

A bridge—there is none—I am alone.

I know. Oh, how better it would be to never have known or seen or felt. Oh, how much better to be a machine. But I see.

I pity me. I am a fool. I need no pity. I am only me. I am, that is enough.

The world goes on.

∞ ∞ ∞ ∞

I love children! I see it more every day—the freshness and exuberance some of us older ones have lost. God has answered some prayers. Still a part is missing.

Only my father can restore that and I will let him take it in his hands. In God is my trust.

I love Jesus!
Nothing.........
I am only one tiny pebble.

∞ ∞ ∞ ∞

As I look out over this world, its people and its problems, I see searching and trouble and sadness. As people search they think they find, but they do not—they have merely become more lost in what they think is right. Each time they lose they have lost more and they fall further into the pit of drugs, hate, war and suffering. There is only one way to climb out of this deep pit and that is with the help of Jesus Christ who came down to Earth and died so that we might know His love and salvation. People laugh at God. They laugh at those who have His salvation; why, I do not know. It is the only thing worth having, the only thing worth being happy for, and yet they laugh and try to turn away those who have it.

As I was walking down the road I was given the key to life (The Word of God). Some take this key and carry it only for a little way then toss it to the roadside. Others reject the key because it is too heavy. Most never accept the key because they think it is dumb and worthless. Those who find the key and carry its weight only a little way find they can use it to open the barrier to Heaven. Beyond this barrier there is only joy.

∽∽ ∽∽ ∽∽ ∽∽

People make things so complicated by trying to figure out why things are and how they got here. They try, with their measly knowledge to discover the answer to things unknown. Yet the answer is not in that direction. It can only be found behind the wall and the only way to get there is with the key. We must be humble and ask God for the help which only He can give, the only real help.

God is not a lot of rules that must be followed, and following the rules will not make you a Christian, because none of us are able to follow the rules. God isn't a chore, He's a friend. He's happiness and peace and He helps us make it through this life so we don't walk in circles. Believe, my friend, Christ is not to be laughed at or to wait for until later or only for Sunday's. He's for now and whenever you need Him.

I was talking to a junkie one day and she said not to knock drugs until you've tried 'em—well, that's what I say about life, "Don't knock it till you've tried it"—about Christ, "Don't knock Him till you've tried Him because He's the only answer."

❧ ❧ ❧ ❧

When I was a child the Lord came to me and said, "Come and follow me." I believed as only a child can believe, but I didn't yet know life and I fell away. Then, one day, the Lord came to me in the wood, the gentle breeze, the lapping of water and said, "Come and follow me." But I paid Him no heed and tread on my path. When the Lord came to me in the form of music, I listened, but didn't know it was the Lord. And the Lord came to me in a friend. I loved the friend, but was too blind to see the Lord. Then the Lord spoke to me in words. I read the book but didn't comprehend. When the Lord came to me through people, I stopped and looked up. Now all is my Lord.

❧ ❧ ❧ ❧

The ultimate choice is there for all to make. However, most never reach that fork. They simply tunnel their way down one well worn path and think that they have made a decision. No, it is necessary to be faced with nothing first in order that something might appear in all its value and worth. The choice is one of happiness or unhappiness. One can look at life long enough and hard enough so as to lose everything and have nothing of worth. That is hell—for then there is no reason or purpose for existence. Yet, existence continues on. It is also possible to find beauty and freshness in all things. This is the road I want to follow but I keep falling off it and wandering away into the darkness. The question that keeps coming to mind is "have I seen too much?" There are so many other worlds inside which I would want to live, but many are ugly and there is much fear hidden in some unknown place. Fear is the most horrible of all for it pulls and scratches and eats away at one until all is swallowed up. Can anything be shared or must all be kept within? The most horrible way to know there is a God is by knowing that life cannot continue on its present course for that would be the greatest of hells. The best imaginable would be an eternal blessed sleep, but existence isn't like that, so, unless there is a God, there is no heaven—only eternal hell.

Have I looked too far to any longer find anything of worth? My heart has seen God and is warm and secure, but my mind is floating in grayness and confusion. Thoughts whirl around so fast that there is no stopping them or they come into focus for only a few seconds and then fade away. The river is moving and heaving all the impurities up onto the shore. Only the heart is pure.

❧ ❧ ❧ ❧

I now understand what it is to have someone else become a part of yourself—and when that part is missing a part of you goes along with it—a longing to again be full exists—no matter how hard I try to pretend it isn't there, it still exists. I must learn to accept reality. It is a wanting, a longing, yet a knowing that what is must be. Existence itself is the greatest miracle, and love in existence is the greatest mystery. Ah, what my heart knows and my mind cannot comprehend. Such are the mysteries of the gifts of God.

What have I learned from music? It cannot be expressed—a great joy and great sorrow, responsibility, honesty, communication. I must learn to be honest and communicate in other things besides music for in other things I feel naked and try to run away. Society and its chains torment me for I am free from them with God. Why do they keep clawing at me? They are so prejudiced. I must either be free or die. I've seen too much of the vastness—far too much.

We are all a part of one another—unity, yet separation.

᷒᷒᷒᷒ ᷒᷒᷒᷒ ᷒᷒᷒᷒ ᷒᷒᷒᷒

I am aware now, more than ever before that the most important thing is love. God created out of love. With Him all is love. We must be unselfish and we must turn to Him for this. We must be patient and sharing and we must turn to Him for this. Good works, without Him, are done only out of self-ishness for we do them because they make us feel good. Only with Him, in whatever form He may come, can we truly love our fellow man.

God says that we must not judge others. Why? Because we will also be judged. Who are we to say that we have the power to tell someone else what is right or wrong with his life? No, each one must follow his own search for God and He will come to each in a particular way. We cannot tell them they are wrong, but we can tell them of the way that has worked for us. There are no limits to God and He can work far beyond the limits of our tiny knowledge. No, only He can enter into some-one's heart and know what is there. We can only know our own—and often not even that.

The human mind is the most powerful of weapons. Within its invention lies the power to build or destroy. Man can use it either to advantage or to disadvantage; he must only choose which. Fear of the mind is the greatest of fears. Many try to run away from using this instrument, because they don't want to chance its great potential. They are afraid that along with the good will come much bad. This is what I also fear, but I have lost the power to run. I have tripped and fallen while try-ing to run away from it. Now it only remains to turn and fight. My mind and body are taken—only heart remains.

83

On Love—

Love is a very precious thing that must be deep inside, because it's the most basic and deep emotion that touches the human being. It cannot be understood or analyzed for it is not logical as is the human mind. But it must be felt inside and allowed to live and grow, not strangled by the human part of us. It must be nourished and watered by God's tender loving care—for only He can build the flower of love. And it must be SHARED. For if love is only kept inside, the flower that God has planted is choked. Love must be shared and communicated always in order to have its full blossom—for love goes beyond the limits of the human body and therefore it can pass from the Spirit of one person to another.

On Music—

The relevance of music lies in its ability to pulsate with life, to speed one's beating heart, make his breathing heavy, and send a chill through one's soul. It is a union, a blending, a penetration between the performer and the listener. The composer creates music in his own image; a reflection of his inner world, and gives this to the performer. The performer then takes this mass of symbols and translates, fills it with his own power, uses it, and enjoys it. The listener receives, lets it fill him, and lets it become a part of his own life. All benefit.

Man can no longer sit on the throne of my life. That place is reserved for only God. I can no longer follow the things man chooses for me to do; I must follow God's rules.

To know is the worst of all. In knowing there is fear, there is worry, there is wondering. To be one that knows, among the free, innocent others. To watch them live in fullness that you know is emptiness. That is the greatest pain. A walk down the road less traveled.

Love, is a gift—from God. It cannot be explained for there are no other reasons than God's, and who can know the will of God? To love, to share, to unite…all is controlled by the Master.

The snow falls, quietly. It wishes to put me to sleep. Silence, peace, warmth. But then the winds come. Sharp, stinging—and I cannot sleep.

There is a time for everything. Be patient. Rest and wait. Grow old.

⁂

I wait, and I wait, and I wait, and as I wait, what I wait for grows farther away.

My typewriter holds 26 letters. Ah, how many words, how many ideas, how many pictures could be formed with them. Yet, the typewriter is empty, for no one is there to use it.

Death, I wait for it to come. I'm so tired. Tired of waiting. Waiting for what? Not death.

The wind speaks to me. It tells me secrets. The secrets of the other worlds. The worlds beyond that no man every shares with another. They are all, alone, in each. And I am, alone, in all.

The pages of time pass by and I watch and wait, a part and not a part. They pass me by and I see myself.

The waters of the river flow so quickly and so slowly. And the voices the river speaks with speak so quickly and so slowly that I cannot understand. Yet I know that I know inside, so I sit and watch and listen as they pass by and I become a part.

Vapor, breath, empty, vanity, nothing. "All is vanity" (Under the Sun). When I lived in "nothing," I knew "nothing." Now I live in "something," and I know both. Two roads—I *cannot* travel both; they both beckon.

The black figure came to me in emptiness and beckoned me, and I wanted not to go, but it pulled me, I went, I saw, I felt—I know "nothing"—I know too much.

To be as a child.

∽∾ ∽∾ ∽∾ ∽∾

All of life is a miracle.

There are no real answers.

This spider web called "life." It pulls, it turns, it strangles. Yet, there is a light up ahead. I keep trying.

∽∾ ∽∾ ∽∾ ∽∾

All of the past is within us, always.

I look at myself now, and know that I am again running. That thing which I hate and despise. I am running from probable pain—running to something much thinner, much easier. And I am afraid, because I know that in the end, what I am running from will win out. I will have to turn and face it, for better or for worse. God must help me.

The snow falls—there are many around me, but my spirit is alone.

∽∾ ∽∾ ∽∾ ∽∾

To truly know a person that person becomes a part of yourself. For who can see into another? In my world on the inside, all are as one; we know one another, without words.

Where is love, without an object? It is empty, without a purpose, and lonely. Where am I, without someone to love? Nowhere. I eat, I sleep, I walk around. But, I am nowhere. I have seen, and it is too late to pretend.

A rose bud
    tender—just beginning to open
A leaf
    pale—just beginning to unfold
A baby bird
    frightened—just learning to fly
A child
    looks at me with big not-understanding eyes

When I don't want to—I must. When I want to—I cannot.
There is no "can't" with God. I can or I will not.

Time—to live beyond time. I worry about time, for I have
to wait, and I don't know what I am waiting for. There is a
place, somewhere, where time will disappear and I will no
longer wait: contentment, peace, and fulfillment.

༄ ༄ ༄ ༄

The instrument—violin—difficult? Yes. Hours of love.
They clap and smile and shake my hand. Maybe even shed a
few tears. They think, "Ah, to be so talented." They see the
lights and the long dress and the calm, poised fingers running
up and down the difficult passages. They think, "Oh, how lucky
she is." They do not know of the pain of tired aching fingers,
years of practice, hours of precision and sleepless nights. A gift?
Yes—a very spectacular and special one. But mostly hard work,
sweat, tears, and pain. Yes, we the chosen must pour in our
love. I want to pour in my love so that they may receive it, and
it may flow between us. I want to pour in my love so that they
may know what I cannot tell them in any other way. I want to
pour in my love so that I may touch their hearts, fill them with
what only this special gift can say. It, the gift, is special, but not
mine—ours. I want them to treasure it, and hold it close, as I
do, and we will share—they and I—we will share in the beauty
of a gift from God.

There is relief, and peace, only when one truly places all one's cares on God. In His hands, all will come to pass as it should. Why am I so stupid? I always wait until the bubble almost pops before I go to Him. Last night we talked, and today is new and fresh. I am happy for I know that my life is in His hands, no matter what comes, He will hold me and help me. *I love You, Jesus!*

I was feeling sorry for myself, and then I looked at the picture of Him in the garden, and knew how much He had suffered, and how much He cared, and how much He wanted to help me. Tears rolled down my cheeks. I must look to Him.

When something difficult lies ahead, it is sometimes scary to have to sit and wait for it. Tonight is a concert, and I am now tense. In a few hours it will be over and I can relax. Only a few hours, to make such a big change in one.

The words that God speaks to me are always full and full of love and help. They always touch my soul in some special way. Human words are sometimes full, but more often empty, full of only the trivial—they leave me empty and searching. That is why I must listen to God.

Follow Jesus, the good Shepherd.

The mark is always there because *I* put it there. I have, within myself, the power to destroy myself. There is no need— God loves me. He has won victory over the mark. All I need do is keep my eyes on Him.

A smile is worth a lifetime. One person is worth a thousand lifetimes.

The way I see often hurts me. Bright, deep, penetrating yet not always true. Usually all is full or all is empty. I live for the few moments of fullness. It changes so quickly. Sometimes all is so bright that it fades into a sheet of grey and I cannot see and don't know if I am walking towards light or dark. All becomes numb and I pretend it doesn't matter.

The practical eludes me—and all becomes a world of dreams, shadowy visions. I float and my skin tingles and I cannot feel, am not a part, only see.

I hate that which is not honest! It so often hurts and destroys. Maybe for a time it protects, but eventually it will fall, and then there is pain.

⁂

My eyes—both warm and cool at the same time. They pierce and dig out the things that are to be covered, filling me with a desire to turn and run the other way. I cannot run from my own eyes. The mirror reveals a mystery to me. I see myself and feel the claws digging in and I feel naked to myself. The mystery is always there, but gone before I discover it, fading into the mists and swirls of fog in my own eyes. It affects me. The moods change, often suddenly, anywhere, at a party, in class, at church, as a jar opening, it comes and pulls me. When I try to follow, it disappears. My eyes hold it, for they are the gateway to the deeper, the other worlds beyond; the worlds I walk through but cannot understand.

The thing is like a figure shrouded in black, foggy and uncertain. It appears and beckons me, then is gone. It is black, not as evil, but as the unknown.

⁂

To argue is to achieve nothing for neither listens and both end up feeling more right and self-righteous. It is better to let the other one talk until he tires of listening to himself.

Conversations and words from the past spin through my mind. They are a part of me—a part of my soul. They affect me, but they move so fast that I cannot touch them. Ah, the power they hold.

I am so tired—my pen moves very slowly across the page. Every muscle of my body is weighed down by the tremendous weight of this tiredness; they fail to respond. My eyelids are swollen thick and very heavy to keep open. I write through almost shut eyes. I do not know where this tiredness comes from for I sleep, and only wake up weaker than before. It is as if, slowly, everything is coming to a stop. There is a dull "something" in my head, not painful, but there—muddying it up, destroying my perceptions and my responses. Tonight I will go nowhere, only just sit, and empty myself of all. I will float away to nowhere and there will be peace and rest—no feeling—no ambition. And then I will come back, and fill up, and be tired again.

Things seem to be escaping from me: my hopes and ambitions, and loves—they are all slipping away. It is not frightening or evil—it is just empty and tired. I simply am—as a shell—empty—except for the tiny corner that I have crawled into. I want to sleep for a time, to rest. When I wake up, they will come back. They are only gone for a time.

Only one flower will ever bloom.

Surface—everything is surface and cold and artificial. I want to crawl deep into the earth and touch what is real—where the colors don't fade when you come close—warmth. And I wish to sleep in that rich reality.

People mean little to me anymore. I don't try to conform. I am different, and I don't care if I fit in or what they think of me. People don't seem real—they are so far away, and I can never trust them. No—they are distant from me—even the closest ones. All they care about are words, words, words! What about truth? They want happiness—don't they know that it isn't really there? Only just stop and live and you will find life—don't go chasing after it.

Feelings seem to stop on the surface—no deeper than my skin. For inside I am tired—too tired.

Books—years of learning and exploring, and ideas—often much garbage.

All is vanity. I hold by a magical thread, only to God.

❧ ❧ ❧ ❧

The cold of the world keeps seeping in—and the snow keeps falling—and the wind howls—and I put on my warmest coat with the big fur collar. But even then, sometimes a tiny sliver of cold pierces its way in and the chill passes through my whole body and it makes me remember how very cold it is outside my coat.

❧ ❧ ❧ ❧

I know they wonder what it is. I catch them staring at me. When I turn to them they look away. Ha! They are weak. Well I won't tell them—even after I find out I won't tell them for they—could never comprehend. Only a few—and I won't tell them for then they would know me and I don't want them to.

❧ ❧ ❧ ❧

Someone to talk with—someone to share with—and I run. Those eyes haunt me—follow me, the ones that could see into me for I hate them to know the weakness inside. Yet, those are the eyes I love, for they are strong and they know even though I pretend. I love them and want to share, but I run and when I turn around again it is too late and I must wait.

Now I walk alone along the edge of the river. It no longer speaks to me but is still—there is no more laughing and no more crying. The birds at one time sang—now they have all flown away. And the wind spoke in the trees and touched my body. Now all is still and the leaves are gone. The snow falls silent—there is no more rain to patter and beat out its mysterious rhythms—only the snow making its sound of silence and the sleeping trees and the hidden river. And now I walk alone in the cold and there is no one laughing beside me, no warm hand in mine—wait for Spring—and I walk, alone, beside the river.

No hate, no pain, no malice, no joy, no laughter, no realness—no love.

❦ ❦ ❦ ❦

Today on the ocean, I met Christ and was filled with Him and I loved Him and we walked and joined the ocean and became the ocean and He filled me and I loved Him and we climbed the mountain and flew over the world and became the wind and He filled me and I loved Him. And I was tired and He picked me up and carried me and I knew He loved me and I knew I trusted Him.

❦ ❦ ❦ ❦

The depth is infinite. I will never find what I am searching for. Then why do I keep looking?

The words fill me and I must write them and keep them.

‹∞› ‹∞› ‹∞› ‹∞›

There is a knot inside my stomach—fear? Nervousness? I don't know. At times it disappears completely and I am filled with peace. I can touch and feel, and there is reality. Then it returns, and all meets, the sparkle disappears and there is dullness in my eyes, all is shadowy and I cannot touch it. I wonder why I am here.

Can I leave anything of value behind? Where is meaning? People float by me and I look into their eyes for one moment—they are confused, afraid, calling for help—and then gone. When the knot appears, I sometimes wish I were dead.

‹∞› ‹∞› ‹∞› ‹∞›

I am a part of the ocean and the sky and the rain, and all that is rotting—the decaying, smelly fish on the beach with their empty staring eyes—and all that is born anew, a baby bird pecking its way out of its shell and wobbling upright. All is me and I am all. I am life and all of life is me—the whole circle, not just the pure, sweet, delicious things but the dark and ugly also. We are all together and share.

WASTE IN ABUNDANCE

Except Love

VALUE IN SCARCITY

‹∞› ‹∞› ‹∞› ‹∞›

I can take nothing with me in the end. I wonder then why I should strive for anything.

Is anything free?

I don't want to give. I want to take.

Union; is there any purpose in union? No—all separates in the end and I am; me, alone, distant.

⚜ ⚜ ⚜ ⚜

Today I wonder, wonder where is the aim and purpose of my life. And I know that it does not matter. I grow every day closer and deeper in contentment. Greatness is everywhere. It does not really matter where I go as long as I live. Jesus holds me. Oh, how I love Him! My heart sings now; I fly with Him soaring above the mountains. He is what matters—and people—He is people. I love people; I care about them, not numbers or points, I really care, I know I do. God tells me to trust in Him, not in things—I rejoice. He is my all!

⚜ ⚜ ⚜ ⚜

The candle burns hidden away. I don't see it now, but it is there, a part of me. I wait, and live, and wonder, and accept. I am content—Jesus cares.

⚜ ⚜ ⚜ ⚜

Empty pages lie ahead and I want to fill them all with songs—the songs that are constantly dancing in my head. They expose a part, a phrase, a note and then fade away until the time is right again. I must sing, write, play. It is bursting inside. When one eats a walnut, one always has to crack the shell first before the meat spills out.

CONTENT…I don't quite understand it. Times come when I am sad and I don't run away; I face, and accept, and go on, and live. The happy times are not phony—they are real. The laughter is real and the tears are real. Jesus is real! I know.

⚜ ⚜ ⚜ ⚜

As I wait, that thing I wait for grows further and further away. What shall I do? Should I sit and wait for it or should I follow and fight for it? Follow?…But, I don't even know what it is.

There is a time and purpose for everything—especially patience.

∞ ∞ ∞ ∞

Today, pictures, and not sounds are important to me. Form, lines, and colors all flash before my eyes. Yet, in a way I do not see, for the pictures are from within.

∞ ∞ ∞ ∞

Children are so special. Not sweet or darling, but something much greater, fresh and honest. Someday I want to have many children, lots of cats and dogs, and a big old house I can bring lonely people home to, people who need hot food and a soft bed—mostly some friends. Also, lots of cupboards and closets for my various collections. And a man whom I can cook for, who likes kids and good hard work, and who likes to play cards, drink beer and go fishing. Also who wears flannel shirts and blue jeans, likes to go for walks in the woods and will sit and listen to me sing; and who will read the Bible for family devotions.

> *God, please touch the things that are wrong, and make them right.*

∞ ∞ ∞ ∞

Pollution—Today—Change—First, Peace.

∞ ∞ ∞ ∞

There is a conflict between what I think out logically and what I feel. My feelings say that God can and will do anything; my mind says He can do anything but probably won't. The things I want are locked into my feelings and my belief in God.

I think the things I think are probably better for me by the world's standards, but they don't move my soul.

Only God doesn't come for a fleeting moment and then pass away. What of the gifts He has given?

I had thought words were inferior; now I know they are precious gifts. I must learn to use them.

Time changes—restless, hurried, impatient, content, peaceful, sleepy. Or do I change?

∽ ∽ ∽ ∽

The sun rises and then falls just as I wake and then sleep. I sometimes wonder what happens on the other side of the world when the sun is there, just as I sometimes wonder what happens to me when I sleep.

∽ ∽ ∽ ∽

She tips over her water cup and then sits sadly nearby. I come to fill it and she wags her tail and slops it up. I tell her to shake hands. She does it slowly as if not sure it will pay off. Then I scratch her behind the ears and she sighs, shuts her eyes, smiles, and enjoys.

∽ ∽ ∽ ∽

I grow so tired of the waiting that my body aches with it, but it is God's will and a part of the plan. I try to forget, but it is always there buried inside. I *know*, just as I *know* God loves me. That *knowing* is the kind that can never go away, no matter how much I use my logic and intellect. And the knowing always shines through in the moments when I am closest to God.

Knowing is the worst of all.
If I didn't know, I would give up.

There is a pain in it all, like a cut that doesn't ever heal completely, but scabs over only to be broken open again by some new bump. Each time, a little more blood is shed and there is always a new tear to take the place of the salty, wet one already crawling down the cheek. The thing has become a part of me, and I can no longer fight it, but merely accept it and live with it, as one learns to live with blindness or a crippled hand. It is always there no matter how much I pretend it is gone. The reality remains. It is a part of me, not cut off, but withered, crippled, and painful. I live, and accept, and wish, and wait.

≈≈ ≈≈ ≈≈ ≈≈

What am I? Not normal. I cannot and will not accept the everyday, run-of-the-mill type of life. Life cannot merely be "good" for me. It must be active and pulsate with vibrance. I have seen that emotions can be real and big and passionate, and I will not settle for less. Not necessarily the "easy" way or the "happy" way, but "my" way, the only way I can go. There is only one road.

≈≈ ≈≈ ≈≈ ≈≈

Time has passed…I have changed…My way of life has changed—the old ones have all gone away, and I have been left with the new ones. They don't know of my ways; they don't understand my ways, so I stay away…. The waiting has changed. It is there, but so deep I cannot feel it, cannot know of its existence, but God knows and cares for it…. My viewpoints, my way of life has changed. Music is my career, but life is my business. I learn, and care for learning…. My touch with God has changed. He is in all my life—not separate. He is my always prayer, not just my special one. He is my whole life, one continuous embrace, not scattered moments of ecstasy.

≈≈ ≈≈ ≈≈ ≈≈

The world is so many colors, and textures, and sounds. Why do we so often not see them but go looking for miracles, when always God holds them out to us?

The rains came this morning and touched me softly. Waiting is almost done, and tomorrow flowers will bloom. The winter is past and much has died. The rain cleans away the garbage and heals the wounds. I live for the rains and today, for tomorrow will come, and I want to be ready.

I have ahead another lesson. I must learn to share. We are united all and we must share. I have been alone for a long time, and have learned much, and it has been good, but the time is coming to be together, and to open up the precious things. I am afraid they will be destroyed by unknowing eyes. I must learn to know when to speak and when to be silent. I have a good Teacher and I trust in Him to know when I am ready.

৵৵ ৵৵ ৵৵ ৵৵

Again it is the time of silence, sleep, loneliness, waiting and I am ready and filled with tiredness. It is good and happy to long and to wait and rest. It is right; my waiting has changed.

৵৵ ৵৵ ৵৵ ৵৵

Another performance. Another aesthetic experience. Another fountain of emotion. Another blossom of talent. Another rain of praise. Another day of work.

> Love—is it a gift?
> in existence outside of man?
> God?
> our creation?
> physical?
> spiritual?
> beyond definition, needing experience.

We must look at what is real, not at what we wish reality to be. Distance, time, changes, experiences separate. Hate and evil are real just as are love and honesty. People are the basis, or is the basis outside of people? Is there existence outside people? Does God exist outside us or is He held within? Why can we not answer realities?

⁓ ⁓ ⁓ ⁓

The end of a time but no end for me. I live always in the new with the old never losing its freshness. All my waiting is over and yet I wait—completely different. There is no longing, no pain, no confusion, only peace and willingness. I have put away many of the childish things, but they are put away in a good way, without regret, without growing old.

I have accepted life and myself and wish to experience them, not to throw them away. To love is to be lonely and to be loved is to never be alone. I am not alone and have shared in much joy and much sorrow in life. He is gone but I am, this time, not alone by the river for to be loved is to never be alone.

Children are the greatest mystery of all to one who views them as children. They are people—if people are a mystery, then they are also, but not in any exaggerated sense.

To be willing to accept a part and not all has been difficult. The incomplete has seemed imperfect, improper. Yet, I've learned that to know the incomplete is full of wonder, discovery, and life; to know the complete is to lose direction, wonder, and much of life. Maybe that is why God wishes to live within us, that He, knowing all, might witness a discovery, a morning, a rising of the sun, a birth.

⁓ ⁓ ⁓ ⁓

Now I really know what this strange peace of God is. It is not only loving God when the good things come but also when the bad things come. God needs and wants our love. Just as we want to be loved when we love, God loves us and wants our love. Love is for all times. We must rejoice and praise Jesus when we suffer. We will be better when we come through it. God's peace and love is not only there for the good times, but also to surround and fill you when you need it most. Read 1 Peter 4.

I can live now. There is no longer reaching for life, but there is *life* in every moment of my being. I don't have to live for the highs; life flows through all. I am changed.

> *I long to go to be with Jesus, but I also long to share this light. Lord help me in every way to live for You. Take my life and use it for You. We will rejoice together—work together—and suffer together—You are my rock—I am your servant.*
>
> *I trust in You, God—not in myself or anyone else. Only You can fulfill my life. You are first—all else must follow. The things I love can only be with me through You. All else will fail. All else is darkness.*

I have spent a long time waiting. For what I never knew and now I have ceased waiting and still don't know if I have found it or what it was. I said once I was marked. I didn't know how or in what way. Now I have lost the feeling of difference and still don't know how or in what way. Once I looked for love and knew what it was and how it existed; now I have found love and have no concept of what it is or how it exists. But now, to live is enough.

The winter is long, the sky dark. The wind is cold, and the river, but as I walked I felt not alone, but healthy in the hard weather.

cᴀᴏ⸱ cᴀᴏ⸱ cᴀᴏ⸱ cᴀᴏ⸱

The center of the goal, the center of the struggle, the center of wanting, the center of pain, and the center of joy is love. We walk alone, each separate, each an entirety, knowing only what we perceive, knowing only ourselves. We are each a Universe. Love—what is it? Who knows it? How can we separate its realities and its imitators? Which is the line where love begins? The center of mankind—and it cannot be touched, cannot be perceived, cannot be explained.

Love is what goes between our separate Universes and makes me *know* that you exist, not only as my perceptions, but alone, full, feeling, thinking, experiencing. Love allows me to know a piece of you, and you to know a piece of me. It is a sharing of self. The goal—to not be alone—is achieved in love.

To love and be loved is the greatest fulfillment. To love and not have love returned is pain. This is why we run from love—this is why we keep relationships shallow and artificial. All have felt the pain to some extent and are afraid of it and run from it. But to take the chance, to face fear, to be willing to sacrifice and to experience true sharing in love, even for a moment, is light and is worth the pain.

God is a part of all this—it is the significance of His creation—it is the breath of life—it is why He could not let man live alone. Two, not one, stay warm in the cold, help each other through bad times, build. Love and sharing are the center of this creation—us.

Jesus suffered and died for us, and His pain was not the pain of nails in His hands and feet and a spear in His side. He suffered the pain of a love for us not returned, that we might never have to know it. He loves us all. He died for us all. He loved us all, even when we hated Him, even when we walked away from Him. That is why Jesus came as a man, so that we would know He felt our pain—not as a God, alien to us, but as a man. The whole importance of knowing Christ lives in this— that He offers us our goal, our wanting, light. He offers us His love, freely, whether returned or not. We have only to love Him and there is fulfillment. There is love given and love returned. This is all—know God—love Him—call Him what you wish—it is the same.

∽∼ ∽∼ ∽∼ ∽∼

Sang at Grandma's funeral—felt her singing along in a chorus of heavenly joy.

∽∼ ∽∼ ∽∼ ∽∼

There is a constant tension in it all and I am used to it and can relax, but those around me who rise and fall in the waves irritate my soul. They try to make me join them and I cannot for I have learned too much.

I must learn sometimes to allow myself to serve music instead of always wanting music to serve me.

Tomorrow I sing and God must touch that song.

> *Lord, let me serve! You, the music, and the*
> *people. Let me be a light for one night—a*
> *focused, directed light—beautiful by your grace.*
> *Thank you, Lord.*

∽∼ ∽∼ ∽∼ ∽∼

I have learned now that to have faith in this God of mine is not a matter of believing in a thing and its happening, but a matter of love. We ask for a thing and then must love our God no matter how He answers. Love is not determined by whether or not things requested come to pass but by itself—love simply is.

Patience and contentment grow out of trying of faith—trying of love. James 1 says that perfection and entirety involves wanting nothing. I have found this to be true. Self-contentment and peace are obtained by wanting nothing. We must accept ourselves and our world. We must love and be pleased with ourselves in order to love and help others. We must not be without goals or opposed to change. Instead we must strive to reach our goals and accept change as a part of life. Acceptance and humility instead of discontent. Revolution and stubbornness, anger even, are fine, but they must be done out of love and humility, not out of hate.

∽ ∽ ∽ ∽

On Reading God's Word—

Remember that all God's words are for life. They are for understanding and appreciation, not merely for knowledge and study. Study the words and then live them and learn them patiently, or they have no meaning or value but are only words and studies, impressive but empty and not solid.

∽ ∽ ∽ ∽

I worry all the time now. There is a constant tension in everything. I'm so tired and my head aches so often. So tired of "taking time," as everyone advises me—there's never any rest. An hour of nothing is filled with guilt—so I delve into something else. There's no time for fun or just for laughs. I fall into bed at night, exhausted, and can't sleep for the things in my mind; often shed tears.

Study fills my time. Learning of facts and ideas—there is no more laughter—but study and thought, logic and sarcasm.

The people around me do and live their halfway and full life—adults are also children, children also adults, and I am alone—never child—not wanting adult. They laugh and I work. It won't continue—I'm so tight—every moment filled with things to do—nothing complete, for when a thing is done, ten others fill its place.

Discontent…I don't want this life. It's not laziness, but a huge weariness—thoughts of years of sunshine spent in darkened rooms and study.

There is fear, this is not of God.

ↀ ↀ ↀ ↀ

Power—to control—to accept the responsibility when others hesitate—to know—to act—to accept the consequences knowing they are worth the result—to decide what is the course of action, leaving others to follow—to set the standard, not for others, but for oneself; they will see and follow—to be aware of truth and lies, real and unreal, concrete and ideological, to use them as tools with full knowledge of their value—to smile when others are fooled. Power: independence to follow one's own ideas; to have them is not enough, one must act.

To use God as an excuse for a nothing, wishy-washy existence is sinful. To pretend He is one's mind, one's decision, one's action is sinful. To place independence of self on the image of God (I say "image" not because I feel God is unreal, but because many see Him only as an image, a reflection of their ideas of Him, and not as He really is), to say "God guides my ways," "God leads my life," "God controls me," "God decides my actions," is living an image, dependence, conformity. Free will is available to all, possessed by few. It is your decision, not God's, your action, not God's, your will, not God's. Accept yourself, live yourself, love yourself, and then you will love God and serve man. Possess, own your own soul, know your goals, wants, and actions and accept them as yours, not any excuses. Others will grab, they will be dependent, slaves, unknowing of their position. They will hinder. Live yourself despite them.

⁓ ⁓ ⁓ ⁓

September 21, 1974

There are many things for which man strives, each his own, each his separate wants. At the end of it all and at the center of it all is one thing: to love and be loved.

⁓ ⁓ ⁓ ⁓

Cris at her lake cabin (age about 17).

Top left: Cristine
on the Texas coast,
age 17.
Above: Cristine
practicing her violin,
age 15.
Left: Cristine with
her mother and Lady
(age about 18)

Cristine's Poems

He Turned on the Light*

When I was a little girl and I was very small,
I walked into a darkened room and couldn't see at all.
Stood up on my toes and stretched out my arm.
To reach the light switch that would keep me from harm.
And then my mama she came and turned on the light for
    me.
And I was so happy 'cause I could see.

And after about a year I walked into a haunted house.
And then I heard a noise that couldn't be a mouse.
And I was very frightened and stood very still.
The darkness crept upon me and gave me a chill
And then my brother he came and he lit a match for me.
And I was so happy 'cause I could see.

And then once there came a night that when I went to bed,
I needed a light shining up above my head.
And the darkness was lonely and I dreamed awful dreams.
And the monster that came made me toss and scream.
And my daddy bought a light that shone through the night
    for me.
And I was so happy 'cause I could see.

Then I grew older and somewhere lost the way.
I always dreaded each coming day.
I tried many things and none seemed to know,
Which way to turn along the road.
And then my Jesus He came and He shone His light for
    me.
And I am so happy 'cause I can see.

* Words to a song written for guitar accompaniment.

Life on a Swing*

A life on a swing that goes nowhere,
A world that's the color of grey,
A place where there are many people,
But the people have nothing to say,
And they turn their face the other way.

Are you lost in the promise of happiness?
Do you ask but the answer is never true?
Then I ask my friend, that you turn around,
There's a hand reachin' out for you—
There's a hand reachin' out for you.

Cause Jesus is a light, that shines in the night,
His love like rain falls to the ground.
And He can fill the spot where love it is not
    with the golden rays of the Son.
His love falls on all,
But only those who call on His name will never
    thirst.
His light as a jewel is waitin' for you,
Just fall on your knees and say—

I'm lost in a chasm of mirrors.
Just show me the one that's right.
I give my life to You, Jesus.
Here's my hand, will You lead me to Your light?
Here's my hand, will You lead me to Your light?

* Words to a song written for guitar accompaniment.

112

There is a struggle in all men
between the outside and the
inside—especially in me.

⤶ ⤶ ⤶ ⤶

I run
To be part of the simple ones
They turn, with puzzled expressions
Not understanding
What is obvious to me
Smiles and words of rain
While I speak of infinity
Practical hands touch my soul
And I plunge into the depths

⤶ ⤶ ⤶ ⤶

When dreams fail,
There is Jesus
To pick up the pieces.

⤶ ⤶ ⤶ ⤶

Time floats by
I learn
I grow
I change and become
What I don't understand
Understanding becomes
Unimportant
As words of life
Compared to living.

⤶ ⤶ ⤶ ⤶

Purple and blue clouds,
Touch a finger to my heart.
Closer and closer…
Darker and darker…
Until they grasp it and,
I cannot get out.

෴ ෴ ෴ ෴

It is thrown out
The door slams/Curses
It is gotten rid of
And tears
Continue to wet the sand…

෴ ෴ ෴ ෴

Buried alive…
I do not panic
But smile
And lay my head down
The weight of the earth
Presses me to sleep

෴ ෴ ෴ ෴

I watched the sun fading in the west window
And knew to see it rise again
I must change my place

෴ ෴ ෴ ෴

One sees a jewel
Draws close to it
Touches it
Fondles it
Holds it close
It raises in one's heart
The desire
To posses it
But one knows
That it is too good
For one.

※ ※ ※ ※

The window faces West
It is my waiting place
I watch the setting sun
Patient
For I know it must rise again

※ ※ ※ ※

To listen to the sounds of…silence.
To walk through the dew filled forest.
The frogs sing in chorus.
And the birds are symphony.
To listen to the sounds…
I walk alone just ahead of them.

※ ※ ※ ※

Dirt
    clings to my shoes
    I cannot scrape it off.
It must wear away.

※ ※ ※ ※

A dark loneliness can truly
Not be shared
For it is empty...
 And there is nothing,
 To share

⸰⊗⸰ ⸰⊗⸰ ⸰⊗⸰ ⸰⊗⸰

To question:
To wander forward in the night
Not knowing that you go
 In circles

⸰⊗⸰ ⸰⊗⸰ ⸰⊗⸰ ⸰⊗⸰

As I sat half-listening,
 in the chapel in the pine,
An itch appeared on my neck.
A wood tick had been
Voyaging. Where to hide him?
 In my pocket?
 In my purse?
 No—he would only crawl out.
Nowhere but between folded hands.

⸰⊗⸰ ⸰⊗⸰ ⸰⊗⸰ ⸰⊗⸰

I had never thought that he would come—not for
    me.
Then one day, he did.
And he smiled to me, and I knew, and he knew.
He took my hand and led me gently through the
    forest,
And taught me new things that I already knew.
We ran and played in the field together,
And it grew dark, and we sat on the hill and
    watched the patterns of the sky.
We listened to the birds together,
And he taught me a new song and a new joy.
He gave me a flower, and we touched it in the
    sunny rain.
Then I wept, and he filled me with strength.
When I was complex, he was simple,
And when I lied, he taught me truth.
And we prayed together and dwelt in the joy of the
    Lord together.
I was his woman and I loved him and he loved me.
Then one day he kissed me and I knew he would
    go.
And he did.
Will he ever come home again?

❧ ❧ ❧ ❧

I do not want to be a flower
Once is enough

❧ ❧ ❧ ❧

The wind passes and the leaves lie still
somber with the wet decay of time.
They come again, always, and the flowers
bloom,
and theirs is a new growth
and fresh water running clear.
Be patient with the setting of the sun
for it shall again arise,
and you will laugh and play in the field
and drink from the clearness of the stream.
Remember the song and hold it close within.

∾ ∾ ∾ ∾

An idea is nothing unless acted upon.
Feelings are nothing unless shared.
Love must be said, not only felt.

∾ ∾ ∾ ∾

A body...
walking, running
working, sleeping
eating, sitting
is nothing
A person
gives a body
life

∾ ∾ ∾ ∾

Language is not as good as...
a look...
a smile...
touch...

∾ ∾ ∾ ∾

A broken bottle
    once fine wine
covered with dust
    stands in a room
where once...
    someone lived.

༺ ༺ ༺ ༺

Perfume
    So strong it gave me a headache
A fly buzzing
    in my eyes
People
    scattered singing
Rays of sunlight
    from the other side
A sermon
    ...too long

༺ ༺ ༺ ༺

    I search
    For what I have
      already found

༺ ༺ ༺ ༺

I sit and I wonder
    Which is best
To run and climb to the highest loft
To laugh and shout
Removing the sliver always hurts
    Or
To sit and wonder

༺ ༺ ༺ ༺

The sea is His
    And it lives for me
The sky is His
    And it lives for me
The earth is His
    And it lives for me
I am His
    And He lives for me.

❧ ❧ ❧ ❧

I reach into the bucket
    Maybe…
        this time
No, there is always a worm
    in it.

❧ ❧ ❧ ❧

Lines
Up and down
Crosswise
Kitty corner
How can I walk straight
When there are so many turns

❧ ❧ ❧ ❧

Together
    with you.
Alone
    is less than alone
It is nothing.

❧ ❧ ❧ ❧

When it was there
     I forgot to say
the words
It remains
I have learned to say
     the words
But
     no one hears.

❧ ❧ ❧ ❧

Pain teaches
     the most beautiful
     of lessons
Just as
     a baby bird
     learns
to fly
     so as to survive.

❧ ❧ ❧ ❧

Love
     is not a question
          of having
Love
     is a question
          of giving

❧ ❧ ❧ ❧

A breeze stirs slowly in the hot, busy city.
It brings the homey fragrance of baking bread.
A pleasant sweetness amid the stinking exhaust
    and sweating people.
I breathe deeply, letting it fill me.
For one moment I am home again. The fields
    stretch before me and I sing and run with
    the earth in my lungs.
Then it is gone…I am once again swallowed up
    in the crowds,
And the breeze settles.

⁂ ⁂ ⁂ ⁂

Pain, we try to make thin.
But, it always is deep.
Like a cut.
Thin and deep.

⁂ ⁂ ⁂ ⁂

eyes are so very important
Not with the seeing
But with the looking inside

eyes are so very important
Not with the looking
But with the seeing

⁂ ⁂ ⁂ ⁂

I asked for the storm
Because I felt brave
I wanted to win through
And stand victorious on top the rainbow
I thought there would be laughter
And jubilation in the end of the battle
But, I am tired of the storm
My eyes are bloodshot from lying
Awake at night listening to its roar
Now, even in defeat, I would
Smile and be glad for the silence.

Sometimes rain falls
On what we call dreams
And washes them
Into a mass of faded color
As an uncovered painting

People change, as leaves
First tiny buds, green and fresh
They grow strong and solid
And then fade to their own special color
And die
Always a part of the whole
They are buried
And return as new buds

I look at the sky
　　It glows
with the dullness of winter.
Snow falls
　　All is silent
Still.
There is a pain in my head
That won't go away
　　Another day

❧　❧　❧　❧

　The words fall
　from tears
　thunder
　and pain.
　They settle
　on trembling earth
　and their mighty force
　is a tender kiss.

❧　❧　❧　❧

There is a girl, dressed in white, sitting in a field of
　　　buttercups
　singing with her guitar and all is quiet.
The birds and squirrels listen and are still; the wind is
　　　silent,
　resting on limbs of trees; we listen.
The many moods of love are held in her song.

❧　❧　❧　❧

Empty words
Fall as rain
Upon bountiful ground.
They are thrust aside.
Winds come.
The stones of hardened faces
Are broken in the storm.
The sun sends its scorching rays
Upon the naked breast.
And it withers.
The land thirsts!
Now the words return
Even as rain does.
The dry ground as a sponge
Drinks them in.
They are no longer empty!

The rickety old cart bumps
and joggles over the
stones.
I urge the driver to go
faster or I will
arrive too late and
the deal will be closed
He smiles a toothless grin
Stops the cart
Climbs down
And whispers in the horses'
ear.
The horse sighs,
He winks at me and smiles
Climbs in
And the rickety old cart
bumps and joggles
over the stones.

1/20/73

THE DUEL

THE ENEMY,
UNBEATABLE!
THE BATTLE,
MUST BE WON!
I DIED LOSING THIS DUEL
MANY DIE,
WITHOUT WINNING.
BUT TOO MANY DIE,
WITHOUT EVEN TRYING.

CRIS REHWALDT

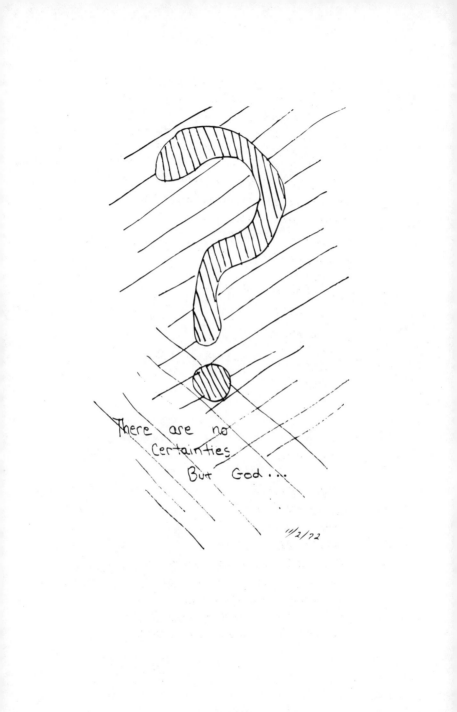

There are no
Certainties
But God...

11/2/72

Cristine

She sang to the world, "Turn, turn, turn."
    She sang, "Turn."
The voice was sweet
Her heart sincere
She sang of Him
Who loved her dear.
"There is a time to live, a time to die."
She knew that well, and yet we cry.
We heard her voice; we see her smile.
The joy she spread; her own sweet style.
To the small child and to the old
Her way was sweet, her heart of gold.
"Can I take her a flower?" a small voice asked.
"She helped me pick cattails;
I want to give her a flower, Mamma.
It will be her last."
A call to the Lord, "Turn. Turn. Turn.
A time to live, a time to learn,
A time to rejoice, a time to mourn.
With love for us all, His Son was born."
This message she sang, this love she lived.
God gave her much, and she did give.
Her talents in life, she used them well
Now at His throne, her soul doth dwell.
Good-bye Cristine, Good-bye dear child
Rejoice with God, rejoice with smiles.
The rose for you, placed by your side
Speaks of the love that will abide.
Our tears do flow, we loved you so!
Your message in life will surely grow
To serve your Savior and praise His worth
While your body lies silent beneath the earth.
A time to weep, a time to mourn.
    Turn, turn, turn.
Listen, dear world, hear her song.
    Learn, learn, learn!

    In memory of my dear niece, Cristine.
    Arlene Prigge

THE BECKONING.

Cristine Rehwaldt

Adagio (♩=56)

Lis —— ten —— to the call —— of the Lord —— and He shall fill thy heart with ma-ny things. —— Lis —— ten ——

for rehearsal only
Piano

Shall all trea-sures o - ver-flow and shall all emp-ti - ness fade a-way.

Shall all trea-sures o - ver-flow and shall all emp-ti - ness fade a-way.

Then
f

Shall all trea-sures o - ver-flow and shall all emp-ti - ness fade a-way

Shall all trea-sures o - ver-flow and shall all emp-ti - ness fade a-way

Then

joy shall reign. Hear — — the call of the Lord. Hear — — the call

and joy. Hear the call of the Lord. —

of the Lord. — — —

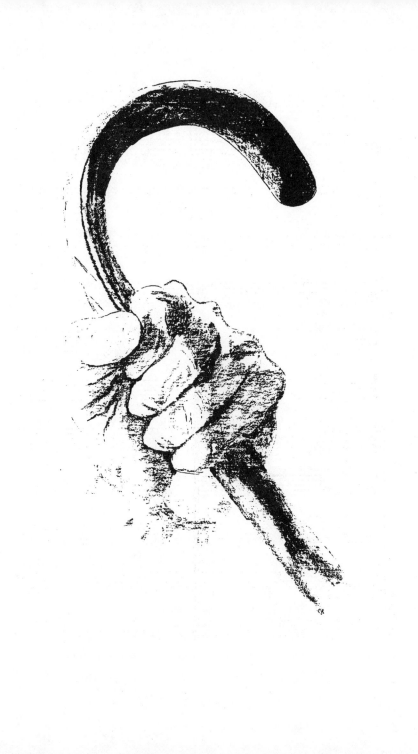